George Glen Napier

The Homes and Haunts of Alfred Lord Tennyson

George Glen Napier

The Homes and Haunts of Alfred Lord Tennyson

ISBN/EAN: 9783743337121

Manufactured in Europe, USA, Canada, Australia, Japa

Cover: Foto ©ninafisch / pixelio.de

Manufactured and distributed by brebook publishing software (www.brebook.com)

George Glen Napier

The Homes and Haunts of Alfred Lord Tennyson

PREFACE.

BEING an admirer of the Laureate's genius, in order to understand the beautiful allusions in his poems, I visited Somersby, Cambridge, Clevedon, Farringford, and Aldworth in the summer of 1888.

It was suggested to me that my tour and the information I had gathered might interest others, so I printed for private circulation, in the spring of 1889, a small book, illustrating it with photographs I had taken in the several localities, and with others kindly given me by friends.

A more generous reception than I had anticipated was accorded to my small volume, accompanied by requests to publish it.

PREFACE.

With a view to doing so, I re-visited the Poet's haunts in Lincolnshire, Surrey, and the Isle of Wight, extending my travels to several other places more or less associated with the Laureate and his work, such as Waltham Abbey, Twickenham, Shiplake, Bolas, and Burleigh, and I now venture to reprint "The Homes and Haunts of Tennyson" in a revised and enlarged form.

I am much indebted to the Hon. Hallam Tennyson, Mr. Horatio Tennyson, and Professor Lushington, who have given me valuable information.

My thanks are also due to Mr. d'Eyncourt of Bayons Manor; Mr. Burton of Somersby; Mr. C. J. Caswell of Horncastle; Dean Gatty of Ecclesfield; Rev. Mr. Soper of Somersby; Rev. Mr. Quirk of Grasby; Mr. Edward Malan of Blackdown, Somerset, and to many others for their kind help.

With regard to the illustrations, let me express my gratitude to Sir George Reid, *P.R.S.A.*, for his drawing of the room in which the Poet was born; Mr. John Murray of Albemarle Street, for the bust of Hallam by Chantrey; Mr. J. E. Mayall, of Messrs. Mayall & Coy., for the photograph of Tennyson taken in 1864 at Farringford. and the Proprietors of the *Graphic* for the study—Aldworth. The photogravures have been engraved by Messrs. Annan of Glasgow.

The compilation of the book has been a source of great pleasure to me, and if it chance to make the study of the Poet's works more interesting my object will have been attained.

G. G. N.

ORCHARD,
WEST KILBRIDE, N.B.,
March, 1892.

CONTENTS.

	PAGE
PREFACE,	v
SOMERSBY.	1
SOMERSBY CHURCH,	19
BAG-ENDERBY,	31
GRASBY,	39
BAYONS MANOR,	61
THE GRANGE AND THE MILL,	77
BURLEIGH HOUSE,	99
IN MEMORIAM,	115

CONTENTS.

	PAGE
MARRIAGE,	151
FARRINGFORD,	161
ALDWORTH,	183

ILLUSTRATIONS.

𝔉ull 𝔓age 𝔓lates.

	PAGE
ALFRED, LORD TENNYSON,	Frontispiece
MAP OF HAUNTS OF TENNYSON.	xvi
SOMERSBY,	2
A SOMERSBY INTERIOR,	16
SOMERSBY CHURCH,	20
BAG-ENDERBY CHURCH,	32
REV. CHARLES TENNYSON TURNER,	40
BAYONS MANOR,	62
GEORGE TENNYSON,	74
SOMERSBY GRANGE,	78
STOCKWORTH MILL,	88

ILLUSTRATIONS.

	PAGE
BURLEIGH HOUSE,	100
ARTHUR HENRY HALLAM,	116
CLEVEDON CHURCH,	132
PROFESSOR EDMUND LAW LUSHINGTON,	142
HORNCASTLE (MR. SELLWOOD'S HOUSE),	152
FARRINGFORD,	162
THE HOME FARM, FARRINGFORD,	180
ALDWORTH,	184
THE STUDY, ALDWORTH,	190

Engravings in the Text.

LINCOLN FROM THE WITHAM,	4
DISTANT VIEW OF SOMERSBY,	5
SOMERSBY BROOK,	10
THE ROAD PASSING SOMERSBY,	12
SOMERSBY GARDEN,	13
THE HALL, SOMERSBY,	15
THE HALL, SOMERSBY,	16
"MY FATHER'S DOOR,"	18

ILLUSTRATIONS.

	PAGE
DR. TENNYSON'S GRAVE,	22
OUTSIDE COVER OF REGISTER OF SOMERSBY,	26
TITLE-PAGE OF REGISTER OF SOMERSBY,	27
REGISTER OF SOMERSBY,	28
ENTRY OF TENNYSON'S BIRTH,	29
INTERIOR OF SOMERSBY CHURCH,	30
VILLAGE OF BAG-ENDERBY,	34
INTERIOR OF BAG-ENDERBY CHURCH,	38
DISTANT VIEW OF LOUTH,	42
"POEMS BY TWO BROTHERS,"	44
THE LINCOLNSHIRE COAST AT MABLETHORPE,	45
MALTBY-LE-MARSH CHURCH,	46
DISTANT VIEW OF CAISTOR,	48
DISTANT VIEW OF GRASBY,	49
GRASBY VICARAGE,	51
GRASBY CHURCH,	56
SONNET—"THE DROWNED SPANIEL,"	57
INTERIOR OF GRASBY CHURCH,	59
TABLET IN GRASBY CHURCH,	60
VILLAGE OF TEALBY,	66

ILLUSTRATIONS.

	PAGE
TEALBY CHURCH,	67
BAYONS MANOR,	71
THE BARBICAN, BAYONS MANOR,	72
TOMB OF GEORGE TENNYSON,	76
"POEMS, CHIEFLY LYRICAL,"	81
A MOATED GRANGE, MALTBY-LE-MARSH,	85
"POEMS, 1833,"	92
HARRINGTON HALL, NEAR SOMERSBY,	95
SCRIVELSBY COURT, NEAR HORNCASTLE,	96
ENTRANCE GATEWAY, SCRIVELSBY COURT,	98
BOLAS, SHROPSHIRE,	104
'THE VILLAGE ALTAR,' BOLAS CHURCH,	105
ENTRY IN REGISTER OF BOLAS,	106
BURLEIGH, NEAR BOLAS,	107
STAMFORD-TOWN, LINCOLNSHIRE,	109
THE LODGE, BURLEIGH HOUSE,	114
CORPUS BUILDINGS, CAMBRIDGE,	118
INTERIOR OF KING'S COLLEGE CHAPEL,	119
THE CAM AT TRINITY COLLEGE,	120
THE WALK OF LIMES, TRINITY COLLEGE,	122

ILLUSTRATIONS.

	PAGE
HALLAM'S ROOMS, TRINITY COLLEGE,	126
INTERIOR OF CLEVEDON CHURCH,	132
HALLAM'S TABLET IN CLEVEDON CHURCH,	135
"IN MEMORIAM,"	136
WALTHAM ABBEY, ESSEX,	138
WIMPOLE STREET, LONDON,	140
PARK HOUSE, NEAR MAIDSTONE,	143
INTERIOR OF PARK HOUSE,	144
CARLYLE'S HOUSE, CHEYNE ROW,	146
TENNYSON'S LETTER TO MOXON,	147
BRANTWOOD, ON CONISTON LAKE,	148
MRS. TENNYSON'S GRAVE, HIGHGATE,	150
HORNCASTLE, LINCOLNSHIRE,	154
CHAPEL HOUSE, TWICKENHAM,	158
SHIPLAKE CHURCH, ON THE THAMES,	160
FRESHWATER BAY, ISLE OF WIGHT,	168
FARRINGFORD LANE,	169
ENTRANCE GATE, FARRINGFORD,	170
FARRINGFORD LODGE,	171
A VISTA, FARRINGFORD,	172

ILLUSTRATIONS.

	PAGE
THE POET'S GLADE, FARRINGFORD,	174
TENNYSON'S DOWN,	176
FARRINGFORD BEACON,	177
FRESHWATER CHURCH,	178
THE NEEDLES,	181
THE "MAYFLOWER" CROSSING THE SOLENT,	182
HASLEMERE, SURREY,	187
TENNYSON'S LANE, HASLEMERE,	188
BLACKDOWN, NEAR ALDWORTH,	191
DISTANT VIEW OF ALDWORTH,	194

Somersby.

"The silent woody places
By the home that gave me birth."

SOMERSBY.

We are accustomed to associate several of the counties of England with certain characteristics of their scenery, Cumberland and Westmoreland with hills and lakes, Durham with coal pits, and Lincolnshire—of which we are about to speak—with fens.

The word fen suggests the idea of a place the reverse of beautiful, hence the preconceived notion of Lincolnshire is that of a region, dull, treeless, level, and uninteresting,

"A flat malarian world of reed and rush!"

Such an opinion regarding the county has prevailed for centuries, and, strange to say, exists at the present time.

Going back to the reign of Henry VIII. we find that monarch calling the county "one of the most brute and beestalie of the whole realm," but in his day there was some ground for giving it such a bad name, as the reclamation of the land by drainage had not commenced. Even after this work had been well nigh completed, the same idea regarding the shire still prevailed, George III.'s notion being that, "it was all flats, fogs, and fens," and coming down to our own day, modern writers such as Hawthorne and Ruskin speak of it in somewhat similar terms.

Now, while it is no doubt true that a great part of the county is very flat, the cloud-capt towers of Lincoln Cathedral being visible for forty miles around, yet if the traveller journey from Lincoln to Horncastle, and thence walk three or four miles eastward, he will find the aspect of the surrounding country completely changed. For, while previously there was nothing that his eye could rest on other than a wide illimitable expanse of flat prosaic land,

"The level waste, the rounding gray,"

now he will survey a pretty pastoral district, where soft wooded hills rise from out deep valleys, down which may be heard the murmur of brooks, hurrying their waters to the German Ocean.

In the very heart of this home scenery, nestling in an atmosphere of tranquil loveliness and rural peace,

lies the hamlet of Somersby, which in all time coming will be noted as the birthplace of Tennyson.

For centuries the estate has been owned by the Burton family, who are lords of the manor and patrons both of its living and that of the adjoining parish of Bag-Enderby.

In the year 1807 there was presented to these

livings a young clergyman of the name of Tennyson, whose father was well known throughout the county of Lincoln as a lawyer and landlord. Previously to his settling here the rector had married Miss Fytche, the daughter of the vicar of Louth, and at the rectory of Somersby,—now the manor-house,—on Sunday, 6th August, 1809, his fourth son, Alfred, the Poet Laureate, was born.

In the quiet country round Somersby the boyhood and early manhood of Tennyson were passed amid what has been called "the cloistral calm of clerical life," and a more fitting place for the upbringing and training of one on whom the Muses had conferred their rarest gifts it would be difficult to find. Outside, in the bright summer days, there was boundless scope for him to wander in solitude, communing with those natural instructors—the trees and flowers, birds and brooks, sweeping plains and "bounding main"; while inside, when frosty winds barred the doors, the long undisturbed winter evenings afforded him ample time for close and applied study, which, under his father's careful tutelage, was the means of laying the foundation of that marvellous knowledge, which drew from Thackeray in after years the encomium that Tennyson was the wisest man he knew.

At the age of nineteen, along with his brother Charles, the poet went up to Trinity College, Cambridge, and while in residence there in 1831, death entered the household at Somersby—his father succumbing to an attack of typhus fever. In many respects the bereavement was a great one, the family losing in Dr. Tennyson one who was not only a pious divine, but a man of deep learning and of large and varied attainments. An old Bentley scholar, he bestowed the greatest care on the education of his family, hence he was revered by those now left to mourn his loss, and by none more than the poet, as his lines referring to this sad event show:—

> This is the curse of time. Alas!
>   In grief I am not all unlearn'd;
> Once thro' mine own doors Death did pass;
>   One went, who never hath return'd.
>
> He will not smile—not speak to me
>   Once more. Two years his chair is seen
> Empty before us. That was he
>   Without whose life I had not been.

For a few years after Dr. Tennyson's death his widow and family continued to reside at Somersby, the ministerial duties being discharged by a curate, the Rev. G. A. Robinson, and many lovely glimpses of the place and of the happy life the poet spent here with his brothers, sisters, and college friends, are unfolded to the reader in the stanzas of "In Memoriam." Take, for instance, the verses where he describes a visit paid by Hallam :--

> O sound to rout the brood of cares,
>   The sweep of scythe in morning dew,
>   The gust that round the garden flew,
> And tumbled half the mellowing pears!
>
> O bliss, when all in circle drawn
>   About him, heart and ear were fed
>   To hear him, as he lay and read
> The Tuscan poets on the lawn :
>
> Or in the all-golden afternoon
>   A guest, or happy sister, sung,
>   Or here she brought the harp and flung
> A ballad to the brightening moon.

Thus the years glided peacefully onwards, the widowed mother leading a quiet, retired life within the seclusion of the old rectory, her sons and daughters growing up into handsome men and women, till 1837, when the Tennysons were obliged to quit Somersby, on account of the new rector, the late Rev. Langhorne Burton Burton, coming into residence.

How dearly Tennyson loved his birthplace, and how sorry he was to leave it, may be gathered from the lines he wrote recalling the period of his departure. One can picture him ascending the hill behind the house and taking a last look at the familiar landscape, or straying down the garden walks and calling back to memory the time when he first heard a voice speaking to him in the wind, and his earliest attempts at poetry, when his brother Charles put a slate into his hand and asked him to write something about the flowers in the garden. But now, alas!

> Unwatch'd, the garden bough shall sway,
>   The tender blossom flutter down,
>   Unloved, that beech will gather brown,
> This maple burn itself away;
>
> Unloved, the sun-flower, shining fair,
>   Ray round with flames her disk of seed,
>   And many a rose-carnation feed
> With summer spice the humming air;

Nor is the little brook which runs at the foot of the garden, and which occurs so often in his poems, forgotten in these musings, and hearing perhaps its sound, he continues—

> Unloved, by many a sandy bar,
>   The brook shall babble down the plain,
>   At noon or when the lesser wain
> Is twisting round the polar star;
>
> . . . .
>
> Till from the garden and the wild
>   A fresh association blow,
>   And year by year the landscape grow
> Familiar to the stranger's child.

Though more than half a century has elapsed since the Tennysons left their early home, Somersby is

situated, happily for us, in such a far away old world region as to be at the present day little, or in nowise altered since the poet wandered along its winding lanes. Time has dealt kindly with the landmarks of the Laureate here, as the hamlets round his birthplace have not grown into villages, nor the villages swollen into towns, but all is delightfully unchanged and rural, due greatly to the fact that it is six miles "an' moor fro' a raäil."

Starting from Horncastle—the nearest market town—the road gradually trends upward for two or three miles, till a ridge is reached which may be said to command the surrounding country. Looking back, we see the smoke rising from the little town just left, and forward the view opens over a beautiful landscape of hill and dale. Eastward the tower of Boston Church can be seen and the glimmer of the Wash; westward "the minster-towers" of Lincoln are in view far away in the distance, crowning the northern heights of the Witham Valley. Point after point, as the road descends, strikes a chord of interest, as the highway is exchanged for that "long acquainted path" leading down "to the dear village haunts" where the poet was born. Great hedgerows shut out the view, but a break in them reveals a little valley, across which may be seen peering out "from the woods that belt the gray hill-side" the chimney tops of Somersby Manor. Descending into the valley, a noise of running water is heard, and a small bridge enables the traveller to cross "the brook that loves to purl o'er matted cress and ribbed sand." The road suddenly curves, then winding up through a deep cutting, reaches the top of the slope, where, separated only by the lusty holly hedge planted by Dr. Tennyson, stands, a few yards back, "the well-beloved place"

under whose red-tiled roof the poet of the Victorian era was born.

The main entrance—what Tennyson calls "my father's door"—is on the side facing the road, but the house as thus approached is not seen to advantage. When, however, it is viewed from the south, where the creepers clamber up the yellow-washed walls, it looks so sweet one does not wonder at the regrets the poet had in leaving such a picturesque home.

The classic lawn, the scene of so many happy gatherings, slopes gently away to a little garden, quaint and old-fashioned, intersected with walks of turf and girt with high evergreen hedges.

In this secluded spot no sounds fall on the ear but those which belong essentially to the pure country—the ripple of the brook murmuring in its summer sleep, the lowing of "the white kine," the bleating of "the thick-fleeced sheep," or the cooing in the distant woods "of the day-long-murmuring wood-pigeon."

The trees add greatly to the beauty of the place, many of the poet's favourites, such as the elms and beeches, still spreading their canopy of leaves over the verdure underneath; but, alas! the "towering sycamore" and "the poplars four" will be no more seen. When Walter White visited Somersby in 1860 he found only three poplars waving behind the house, as one had disappeared; now all are gone—in Mr. Rawnsley's choice language, "they only whisper in the Laureate's song."

As for the interior of the old manor-house, it may be said to have all the peculiar charm of an English country home. The ivy-mantled door opens on a square hall, adorned with many tokens of the chase, crossing which we enter the drawing-room rich with pictures, china, and a wealth of bric-a-brac. It is charmingly sunny, being lit with two large windows on a level with the lawn, and for cheerfulness is quite a contrast to a somewhat dingy room on the opposite side of the passage, which must have been associated with sad memories, as in it Dr. Tennyson died.

Passing along a dimly-lighted corridor, a pointed gothic door opens on the dining-hall. This apartment is one of stately dimensions, having been designed by the rector himself, who, to his many other accomplishments, added a thorough knowledge of architecture, the groined roof and high ecclesiastical windows, the beautifully modelled mantelpiece and

carved panelled door all attesting his refined and excellent taste.

To this hall Tennyson makes reference in "In Memoriam" as that in which the family were wont to gather on festive occasions, and doubtless its old walls full many and many a time "with harp and carol rang," more especially at Christmas, when the poet and his brothers came down from Cambridge, accompanied by some of their college friends, to spend the vacation at Somersby—

> As in the winters left behind,
>   Again our ancient games had place,
>   The mimic picture's breathing grace,
> And dance and song and hoodman-blind.

Such scenes of mirth and merry-making were not always suited to the poet's habits of solitude—manifest even at this early age—and oftener than elsewhere was he to be found alone with his books in his

SOMERSBY.

The Room in which the Poet was born.

study in the attic. A private stair, rather dark and difficult to climb, leads up to it from the ground floor; but the sanctuary of the Muse is strangely altered, and the lines the poet addressed to it—

> O darling room, my heart's delight,
> Dear room, the apple of my sight,
>   .   .   .   .
> No little room so warm and bright,
> Wherein to read, wherein to write—

would hardly describe it now, as the books which lined the walls and gave to it such a cheerful look have been superseded by "Lincolnshire Pictures."

The skylight has been closed in, and now only one window in the gable-wall greets the day, the view from it embracing a wide prospect over the wolds.

Our chief interest, however, centres in the room in which the poet was born. It is over the drawing-room, and is distinguishable by the iron balcony in front of its window, but the aspect of the interior is greatly changed, owing to the furniture being altogether different from that of eighty years ago.

Standing in this room our thoughts naturally travel back over the years to that memorable day when the roofs above heard the poet's "earliest cry."

Somersby would then be at its loveliest, for the Laureate was born on what Charles Lamb would call "an all-day day" in August, that charming month when summer, falling into the lap of autumn, "gilds the glebe of England."

Little would his parents think that to their house had just been born an "heir of endless fame," yet it was so; for the voice first heard within these walls will never die, but continue ringing down the corridors of Time, and like the echoes in the "Princess,"

> roll from soul to soul,
> And grow for ever and for ever.

Somersby Church.

"Like soften'd airs that blowing steal,
When meres begin to uncongeal,
The sweet church bells began to peal."

Somersby Church.

SOMERSBY CHURCH.

WHEN depicting in the poem entitled "The Two Voices" the struggle which constantly goes on between the intellect and heart of man, all will remember that Tennyson causes the latter to triumph over the former by the joy awakened at the sight of happy people gathering on a Sabbath morning for divine service.

> I ceased, and sat as one forlorn.
> Then said the voice, in quiet scorn,
> "Behold, it is the Sabbath morn."
>   .   .   .   .   .
> On to God's house the people prest:
> Passing the place where each must rest,
> Each enter'd like a welcome guest.
>   .   .   .   .   .   .
> I blest them, and they wander'd on :
> I spoke, but answer came there none :
> The dull and bitter voice was gone.

It is not too much to suppose that "God's house" here referred to is Somersby Church, as the scene which the poet describes must often have been witnessed by him in his boyhood as his father's parishioners assembled for morning worship.

Ten yards past the manor house, on the opposite side of the road, a small wicket gate, hidden under

the shade of trees, opens to a narrow path, ascending which we enter the churchyard of Somersby.

All things here have rest; absolute stillness reigns.

SOMERSBY CHURCH.

It is truly a country churchyard, its beauty in no way destroyed by huge blocks of granite and marble, but here and there lichen-covered headstones with simple inscriptions telling of lives "lived and ended honestly."

Under the shade of the rugged little church-tower sleeps the poet's father. The tomb is enclosed by high railings, the altar slab bearing the following inscription :—

TO THE MEMORY OF
THE REVEREND
GEORGE CLAYTON TENNYSON,
LL.D.,
ELDEST SON OF GEORGE TENNYSON, ESQ.,
OF BAYONS MANOR,
AND RECTOR OF THIS PARISH,
OF BAG-ENDERBY AND BENNIWORTH,
AND VICAR OF GREAT GRIMSBY
IN THIS COUNTY.
HE DEPARTED THIS LIFE,
ON THE 16TH DAY OF MARCH, 1831,
AGED 52 YEARS.

The poet, thinking of his father lying here, while his family are far removed from him, refers to this tomb in these lines :—

> Our father's dust is left alone
>   And silent under other snows
>   There in due time the woodbine blows,
> The violet comes, but we are gone.

So remote is the district, the church and churchyard seem to have escaped the vigilant eyes of the Puritans, when they hurried to and fro throughout the land laying forcible hands on all popish images, and accordingly there are still to be found here traces of *pre*-Reformation times.

One of these relics, almost unique in its complete preservation, is a Norman cross, with a figure of our Lord on one side, and the Virgin on the other; while close to the entrance of the church, in a dark corner, is a little flat stone basin for holy water. Though trees circle round the churchyard, there is no "dark yew" among them, neither is there a clock in the tower to beat out "the little lives of men," the only recorder of the hour being a sundial over the porch, with date 1751, and motto "Time passeth."

The church must have been a very quaint edifice in Dr. Tennyson's time, as its roof was then covered with thatch, like the cottages in its immediate vicinity. The tower is the oldest portion of the building, and in several places has been patched with red bricks instead of stone.

It contains two melodious bells whose soft tones must often have fallen upon the poet's ear.

"Would'st thou know the beauty of holiness?" says Charles Lamb. "Go alone on some weekday, borrowing the keys of good Master Sexton, traverse the cool aisles of some country church; think of the piety that has kneeled there—the congregations, old and young, that have found consolation there—the meek pastor, the docile parishioner."

With emotions akin to what Lamb here describes we open the ponderous oaken door of this 'pastoral sanctuary,' but a feeling of disappointment is experienced, as the interior does not at all harmonize with what the exterior would lead one to expect. This part of the church has been restored, regardless of congruity—the new pews and coloured tiles ill-assorting with the old weather-beaten walls. One thing remains unchanged, "the cold baptismal font," octagonal in shape, and of plain freestone, where, according to the register of Somersby, on Tuesday, the 8th August 1809, two days after his birth, the poet received the name of Alfred.

It is matter for thankfulness that so many parish registers have come down to us preserved from the decay of Time and other destructive influences.

Whatever mist may envelope Shakespeare's life, no

doubt can exist as to the date of his baptism and burial, thanks to the parish register of Stratford, which lies open to the gaze of the world in the church which contains the poet's dust.

Under a similar debt of obligation are we laid to the quaint old register of Somersby, containing the birth and baptism of Tennyson, as from a perusal of its pages we are enabled to ascertain certain definite facts of considerable value regarding the poet and his family.

The book, which is the second Register of Somersby, is deposited in the rectory at Bag-Enderby, and is in excellent preservation. The leaves are made of thick parchment, same as the outside cover, which bears the date 1735.

SOMERSBY CHURCH.

A predecessor of Dr. Tennyson (the Rev. Ralph Battell) must have been a skilful penman, as he commences the volume with a title-page of no little beauty, describing the contents as "a Register of all the Births, Burials, and Marriages belonging to the parish of Somersby, in the County of Lincoln,' etc., etc.

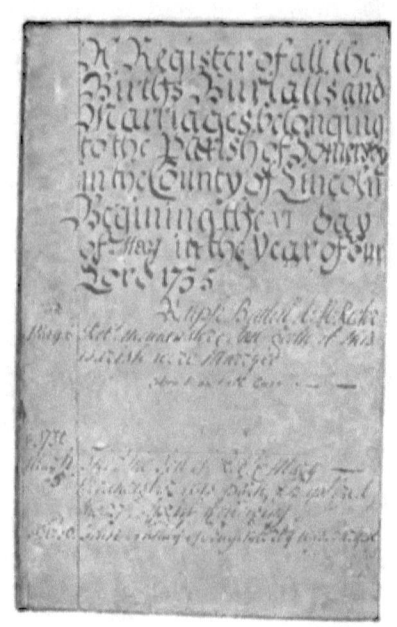

The first entry in Dr. Tennyson's handwriting is to be found on the bottom line of the page previous to that which contains the birth of the poet. The date is June 14th, 1807, the entry above it, May 6th, being signed by Jo⁺ Younghusband, curate, whose name also appears at the end of the years 1802, 1803, and 1806.

From June 14th, 1807, to June 28th, 1808, a whole year elapses without a single entry in the Register.

SOMERSBY CHURCH.

At the top of the page, containing the years 1808, 1809, 1810, and portion of 1811, the name of the Rev.

G. C. Tennyson as rector occurs for the first time. The third entry in the year 1808 records the birth, on July 4th, of Charles Tennyson, and his baptism on July 10th; the last entry in the same year being the baptism on November 3rd of the late Rev. Langhorne Burton Burton, father of the present owner of Somersby, and successor of Dr. Tennyson in the livings.

It is somewhat remarkable that of all the entries in Dr. Tennyson's elegant caligraphy in this book the only figure open to doubt is the date of the birth of the poet.

It is the third entry in the year 1809, and runs as follows :—

[handwritten entry: Augt. 8. Alfred son of George Clayton & Elizabeth Tennyson bapt. born Augt. 1549]

At the first glance the last figure looks like a 5, but on closer examination it proves to be a 6, the difficulty in reading the entry being caused by this figure being made above the line and close to the inner convex, or rounded margin of the old Parchment Book. That this is correct may be said to be beyond doubt, Lord Tennyson's authority having recently been given, that, according to his mother's testimony, he was born on the 6th of August, which, it is worth noting, was the fourth anniversary of his parents' marriage.

The birth of the poet's eldest sister, Mary, is recorded in 1810, while that of Emilia in 1811 is the last entry in this Register relating to the Tennysons. On 29th December, 1812, in the centre of the page opposite the entry of the poet's birth, the rector closes the book with these words—"Here commences the new Register established by Act | of | Parliament," and in the new volume are recorded the baptisms of the younger members of his family.

Bag-Enderby.

"Enormous elm-tree-boles did stoop and lean
 Upon the dusky brushwood underneath
 Their broad curved branches, fledged with clearest green,
 New from its silken sheath."

Peag-Sudnly Church.

BAG-ENDERBY.

A FEATURE of this part of Lincolnshire is the nearness of the villages to each other, as is shown by the poet hearing at one time the Christmas bells ringing from four of the neighbouring churches.

> The time draws near the birth of Christ :
> The moon is hid ; the night is still ;
> The Christmas bells from hill to hill
> Answer each other in the mist.
>
> Four voices of four hamlets round,
> From far and near, on mead and moor,
> Swell out and fail, as if a door
> Were shut between me and the sound :

Not long ago the rector of Somersby received a letter from an American, asking him what four hamlets the poet here refers to, and Mr. Horatio Tennyson, who happened to be staying in the vicinity, promised to make inquiry of his brother. The poet's reply was that he had forgotten, but there can be little doubt that one of the four is Bag-Enderby, as it is only half a mile distant from Somersby.

The livings have always been held conjointly, service being conducted in the morning at one church and in the afternoon at the other.

It may be noted that these parishes are called hamlets, which word exactly describes them, as they consist of only a few scattered cottages. At Bag-Enderby these are ranged on each side of the roadway, and form a sort of village, the entrance to which is guarded by a great elm-tree.

There is a difference of opinion as to which is the poet's favourite tree, some careful students of his poems maintaining that it is the chestnut, others that it is the elm. Possibly it is neither, but in favour of the latter it may be mentioned that in the poet's native county the elm is a very common tree, the strong clayey moist soil of Lincolnshire seeming to be specially adapted to its requirements.

It is a tree remarkable for the great horizontal limbs which it throws out, sometimes to a distance of thirty or forty feet from its trunk, and the elm at Bag-Enderby is a good instance of this peculiarity, as one of its boughs, on which the poet's sisters used to swing in their girlish days, is now so large as to afford, it is said, sufficient accommodation for the whole of the population of the parish to sit side by side on it in comfort.

There are three Enderbys in this vicinity—Mavis, Wood, and Bag-Enderby. The prefix Bag—which occurs in old Lincolnshire Records as far back as 1220—has been rather a puzzle to antiquaries, and would have deserved the researches of Jonathan Oldbuck. One interpretation is that Bag is a corruption of Beck, the local name of the rivulet which flows along the foot of the valley; another, that it is the old Norse Bak, which, rendered into English, means Back; while the fact that Badgers are to be found in the holes of the sandstone rocks in the immediate neighbourhood has given rise to the belief that possibly the prefix may have been derived from these animals.

The church stands at the end of the village, and at first sight might be mistaken for a ruin, as the old pointed roof has been removed, leaving the bare gable. As far as can be ascertained, the edifice was built in the middle of the 14th century, when it was dedicated to St. Margaret. Internally it is much more interesting than its neighbour at Somersby, the little high-built pulpit where Dr. Tennyson read his sermons, and the great square squire's seat in which the poet sat and listened to them, being entirely unchanged. The baptismal font (at least 500 years old) is quite a contrast to the one in Somersby Church, as it is as elaborately carved as the other is plain, one of its devices, strange to say, being a poet playing on a harp.

There still resides in Bag-Enderby an old man, by name Jonathan Clark, who was born there in the same year as the poet, and is now one of the few survivors of these bygone days. Bent nearly double with age, he still manages to hobble from church to church, in order to discharge his duties of clerk and 'clinkumbell.' He is 'a mine of memories,' having many reminiscences to relate of his boyhood, though it is to be feared his imagination is at times a ready mint for the coinage of some of his stories.

"The doctor wur all for reading," is his summing up of Dr. Tennyson's character, a remark not wanting in truth, as the poet's father's tastes were somewhat akin to those of the rector described by Crabbe, whose delight

> "Was all in books; to read them, or to write:
> . . . .
> Courteous enough, but careless what he said,
> For points of learning he reserved his head."

Jonathan distinctly remembers the Misses Tennyson, "young ladies who were never seen without a book in their hands," and the rector's seven tall sons; but he has no special recollection of the poet, as at that time he was not "nobly distinguished above all the six."

The old man declares that some twenty years ago he drove the poet over from Alford to Somersby, but herein his memory fails to note the flight of time, as the Laureate might say with Matthew Arnold,

"Too rare, too rare, grow now my visits here,"

not having been in the locality for nearly forty years. Still, though the poet has not visited his birthplace for so many years, it is a mistake to think his interest in his native district has ceased, for, as his brother once remarked, the writer of "Tears, idle tears," never could forget Somersby.

Grasby.

"True brother, only to be known
By those who love thee best."

GRASBY.

NOT unfittingly has the young household at Somersby been compared to a nest of nightingales, as most of the sons seem to have inherited the poetical gifts of their father.

Frederick, the eldest, is the author of three volumes of poetry, entitled "Days and Hours," "The Isles of Greece," and "Daphne and other Poems," while Edward, Septimus, and Horatio have each written verses more or less known. Though some, however, might gainsay the claims of these to be called poets, few will deny the title to their brother Charles—indeed, all who have studied his sonnets feel that no lines could better describe his genius than those which the Laureate caused to be cut on the mural tablet he erected to his memory in Grasby Church:—

"True poet, surely to be found
When Truth is found again."

Charles Tennyson was the first of the rector's children born at Somersby, being little more than a year older than his brother Alfred. From their

infant days till early manhood the two were constant companions, running side by side for many a mile in their race after the Muses, till at length the one shot far ahead, completely distancing the other. No one was more ready to acknowledge this superiority than the elder brother;—in fact, his willingness to take the second place is noticeable in the earliest glimpse we get of him.

After spending four years at the Grammar School

of Louth, "one of these old classic institutions," says
de Quincey, "which form the peculiar glory of Eng-
land," the brothers returned to Somersby—the next
six years being spent in studious retirement at their
father's rectory. During this time they were ex-
tremely diligent, encouraging and helping each other
in their literary studies, "drawing blood" from the
books they read, which in point of number cannot
have fallen short of those which their predecessor
Byron tells us he had mastered at a similar age. A
few years later we find Charles Tennyson writing a
sonnet on "Perseverance," which no doubt reflects
the earnest way they grappled with those difficulties
that beset the path of every student.

> "On, on, in firm progression, sure and slow,
>   More scorning hindrance, as ye meet it more;
> Surmounting what ye cannot thorough go,
> And forcing what ye fail in climbing o'er;
> Soon shall ye gaze upon the bliss attained,
> And worth attainment fourfold as severe;
> The glorious meed for zealous souls ordained,
> Shall shine upon you, palpable and clear;
> Then when the starry coronal of Fame
> Shall gird your brows, all-perdurably bright;
> When ye have seen the solitary flame,
> That burns upon the solitary height,

        Ye will not, then, your daily cares misname
        As toil—well spent, for rapture to requite!"

In their case, "the bliss attained" may be said to have been the publication, near the close of the year

1826, of 'Poems by Two Brothers,' a volume which, in spite of their time being so fully occupied, they found leisure to write "from the ages of fifteen to eighteen."

Messrs. Jackson, of Louth, were the publishers, purchasing the copyright for £20, which price can hardly have been a remunerative one, as the book was as

little sought after then as it is eagerly enquired for
now. Yet, little as may have been the notice the
volume attracted in the republic of letters, its appear-
ance was an event in the lives of the young Tenny-
sons—the day on which they first donned the livery
of the Muse being memorable to them. Many years
afterwards the elder poet recalled this glad time,
relating to the Rev. H. D. Rawnsley how he and his
brother in their joy took carriage from Louth the
afternoon the book was published, and driving across
the marsh to Mablethorpe

> "to the ocean gave
> Their mind and thoughts, as restless as the wave.'

Before returning to Somersby
the young poets, like dutiful sons of a clergyman, spent
their hardearned money in a tour through Lincolnshire
inspecting the different churches, for which the county
is so justly famous. Those in the marsh would probably

first be visited (of which that at Maltby-le-marsh may be taken as a type), stately old gray-stone edifices with walls covered with ivy and square towers keep-

ing watch over the graves of buried generations. Listening to the bells of some such church, Charles Tennyson writes—

"Follow the sound, and it will lead thee on
Into an English church, the home of Prayer.
For who shall say she is not lovelier there,
Than in all other fanes beneath the Sun?
There, if thou doubtest, may it not impart
Fresh hope, to learn that others' hope is sure?
There, duly as the merchant to the mart,

> Come aged men, whom daily death makes fewer ;
> There all the spirit of a Christian heart
> Is bodied forth in gentle rites and pure."

Some of the brightest intellects of our century, men whose names through their works are household words, have, after a brilliant college career, passed their lives in a quiet rural parish.

Keble, Kingsley, and Charles Tennyson may thus be linked together, from the similarity of their attainments, the choice of their profession, and the manner of their after lives.

When a student at Oriel no one was more looked up to than the author of "The Christian Year," yet Keble retired from the intellectual society of Oxford to spend the rest of his days preaching and ministering to the farmers and hinds of Hursley.

Kingsley at Magdalen astonished his tutor with the way in which his mind grasped the most abstruse questions; but abandoning the idea of a lucrative profession, the author of "Westward Ho!" decided for the Church, passing the remainder of his life as rector of Eversley.

A somewhat similar life was Charles Tennyson's. At Cambridge, owing to his having gained a Bell scholarship and published a volume of sonnets, he became a marked man, mixing among the exclusive set of the superior minds of his University, and winning the approval of Wordsworth and Coleridge. But all ambitious literary hopes he laid aside, and betaking himself to the study of divinity entered into holy orders and was ordained curate of Tealby in Lincolnshire.

Eight miles north of Tealby stands the old Roman-

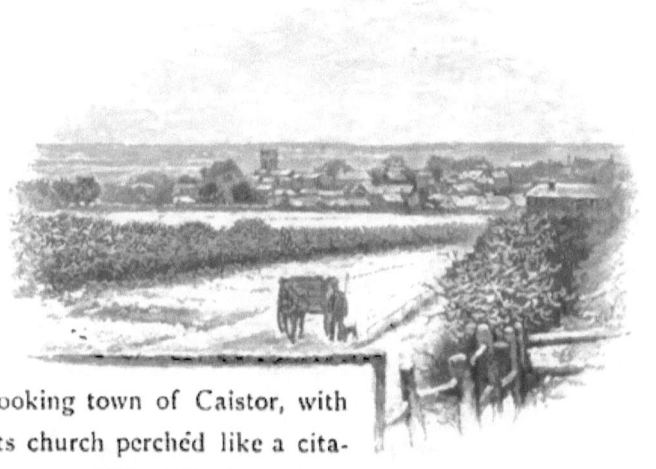

looking town of Caistor, with its church perched like a citadel on a hill. The Rev. Samuel Turner, great-uncle of the Tennysons, lived here some 60 years ago, occupying a large mansion in the square. His grandnephews being special favourites with him, were frequent denizens of this quaint town, "so much so," says Cuthbert Bede, "that to this day, the Caistorians proudly call the Poet Laureate 'our poet,' declaring that it was within hearing of their church bells he wrote his exquisite poem 'The Death of the Old Year.'"

Though Mr. Turner resided in Caistor, he was not

rector of that town, but vicar and patron of Grasby, a little village (on which it is said the sun never sets) nestling some three miles distant on the Lincolnshire wolds.

To the estate and living of Grasby, Charles Tennyson succeeded in the year 1835, taking by royal license the surname of Turner under the direction of his great-uncle's will, and the following year he married

Miss Louisa Sellwood—the youngest sister of the lady who became the wife of his illustrious brother.

As a considerable time had elapsed since the publication of his sonnets at Cambridge, Mr. Turner's friends naturally looked forward to a recurrence of poetical activity, now that he was settled with his young wife in such pleasant surroundings; but year followed year, decade decade, and not a line came from his pen. Far off echoes from the great world told him how his brother was now threading

> "the secretest walks of fame,"

but such tidings, instead of raising a ripple of jealousy in his mind, were rather a stimulus to him, as he was much more interested in his brother's success than his own. Like Sir Percivale, the young vicar of Grasby

> "Had pass'd into the silent life of prayer,
> Praise, fast, and alms,"

the joys and sorrows, hopes and fears, of his parishioners entering deeply into his pitying heart and engaging all his sympathies. For them he seemed unable to do enough, labouring incessantly, with his good wife, for their welfare—the use of his carriage, the milk of his cows, his wine, his coals, being freely given to those in need—while even the

privacy of his vicarage was not denied them, as under his own roof he delighted, on a winter's evening, to gather his flock and teach them, like the Pastor of Woldsby Ebriorum, by "words and books." On such occasions, to hear him read the "Queen o' the May," and "Break, break, break" was a treat never to be forgotten, the tears rising in his eyes, as in slow and measured tones he repeated the last two lines of the latter poem—

> "But the tender grace of a day that is dead
> Will never come back to me."

"Pray, think, and strive! with God's good Book for guide," may be said to have been his motto, while his creed was one "of love, and faith, and holy fear"; and thus, spending and being spent, the summer of his life went quietly past, moving, as he tells us, "in modest round among my neighbours"—

> "Thro' troops of unrecording friends,
> A deedful life, a silent voice."

But though his mellow voice was so long hushed, the muse had not wholly died within him, the autumn of his life bearing as much fruit as the poetic blossom of his youth had foretold. Within the space of ten years (1864-73) well nigh three hundred sonnets came from his pen, exhibiting all the old grace, power, and kindliness of spirit trebly intensified.

A "Saviour-tone of love" breathes throughout these sonnets,—kindly, pious thoughts being sure to rise in the minds of those who read them, as no verse is more touching, none more genuine or worthy of study. Like Burns, our poet lives in sympathy, his heart overflowing with love, not only for human beings and animals, but even for inanimate creation.

To understand how beautifully this gentle trait in his character finds expression in his sonnets one has only to read those addressed to "The Buoy-Bell," "The Old Rocking-Horse," and perhaps best of all, "To a Scarecrow, or Malkin, left long after Harvest."

> "Poor malkin, why hast thou been left behind?
> The wains long since have carted off the sheaves,
> And keen October, with his whistling wind,
> Snaps all the footstalks of the crisping leaves;
> Methinks thou art not wholly make-believe;
> Thy posture, hat and coat, are human still;
> Could'st thou but push a hand from out thy sleeve!
> Or smile on me! but ah! thy face is nil!
> The stubbles darken round thee, lonely one!
> And man has left thee, all this dreary term,
> No mate beside thee—far from social joy;
> As some poor clerk survives his ruin'd firm,
> And, in a napless hat, without employ,
> Stands, in the autumn of his life, alone."

The personality of the writer is constantly present in his pages, affording the reader an insight into his life and work at Grasby, supported and solaced as he was by the hopes and exercises of religion. Like a true pastor he dwelt much at home; still no one was more fond of travel, and on his return to his calm retreat he wrote many sonnets incidental to the events which happened to cross his path when travelling in Italy, or making a circuit of visits among his friends in England and Wales.

The pleasure he derived from a sojourn at Farringford is evident from his "Farewell to the Isle of Wight," a sonnet which shows that years of separation, instead of diminishing, rather enhanced the affection which existed between the poet-brothers.

> "my memory wander'd back
> To those fair shores—the Needles and the Downs
> The happy woodlands and the little towns—
> For every day a new and pleasant track;
> How grieved was I those social walks to lose,
> Those friendly hands !   .   .   .
>   .   .   those fond adieus."

In contrast to this grief at parting was the joy he experienced when his brother was a guest at the vicarage. These visits were rare, as the Laureate did not often come to Grasby, but when he did, they were halcyon days in the life of the vicar. The social walks were then renewed, their boyish and college memories recalled, while the many subjects they had in common, such as their love of astronomy, ornithology, arboriculture, etc., supplied them with endless topics of conversation.

It was on one of these visits that the Laureate witnessed a village school feast—which, as Mr. Spedding in his delightful essay on Mr. Turner's life and genius tells us, was the most stirring and picturesque event connected with the pastor's round of duties.

> "The Feast is o'er—the music and the stir—
> The sound of bat and ball, the mimic gun;
> The lawn grows darker, and the setting sun
> Has stolen the flash from off the gossamer,
> And drawn the midges westward; youth's glad cry—
> The smaller children's fun-exacting claims,
> Their merry raids across the graver games,
> Their ever-crossing paths of restless joy,
> Have ceased—And, ere a new Feast-day shall shine,
> Perchance my soul to other worlds may pass;
> Another head in childhood's cause may plot,
> Another Pastor muse in the same spot,
> And the first dews, that gather on the grass
> Next morn, may gleam in every track but mine!"

During the years of his ministry he built the vicarage and schools, and rebuilt the church, the cost being entirely defrayed by himself. The pleasure he took in this work is evinced from his sonnets on "Our new Church," and "Our new Church Clock,"

—in the latter of which we see another proof of the vicar's anxiety to do all in his power to brighten the lives of those around him:

"How sweet at eventide
Will that clear music be to toil-worn men!
Calling them home, each to his own fire-side;
How sweet the toll of all the hours till then!"

In the spire he placed two bells, one to the memory of his mother (whom he was said to resemble more than any of his brothers), the other to his father-in-law, Mr. Sellwood.

His health failing him, he came north to Scotland, and was much benefited by the bracing sea air of the Ayrshire coast. Though weak in body, his mind was as vigorous as ever, and he there wrote many fine sonnets, one—that on "The Drowned Spaniel"—being inspired by the poet finding a poor drowned dog as he was strolling over the sandy beach near Ardrossan.

> *On finding a Spaniel*
> *drowned by the Seaside*
> *after a Storm.*
>
> The daylong bluster of the storm was o'er,
> The sands were bright. The winds were all asleep
> And from the far horizon, o'er the deep
> The sunset swam unshadow'd to the shore;
> O'erhead the Rainbow had not pass'd away,
> When, roving o'er the shingly beach, I found
> A little waif, a spaniel newly drown'd—
> The shining waters kiss'd him as he lay.
> "In some fond heart his gentle memory dwells,"
> I thought; and, though thy latest aspect tells
> Of drowning pains and mortal agony,
> Thy master's self might weep & smile to see
> His little dog stretch'd on these oozy shells,
> Between the Rainbow and the golden Sea.

Whilst residing in Ayrshire he made a pilgrimage to the birthplace of Burns, as he was a warm admirer of the poems of Scotland's national poet. Perhaps the

"Scotch Song" in "Poems by Two Brothers," might be traceable to this affection for the poet, although no further attempt at versification in Burns' mother-tongue was again tried by either of the brothers.

In "Euphranor" Fitzgerald tells us how the Laureate broke into a passion of tears when he found himself beside the 'Bonnie Doon,' and the same sympathetic feeling for Caledonia's bard is observable in Mr. Turner's sonnet on the "Localities of Burns."

> "When the bright crescent gleam'd o'er hill and dale
> We saw the poet's lowly place of birth,
> The Kirk, erewhile the scene of fiendish mirth,
> The brig that parted Maggie and her tail.
> We saw his bust, we saw the cenotaph,
> Which on the skirts of that fair garden stands,
> And Tam o' Shanter with his soundless laugh
> Over his empty cup and stony hands—
> All these were present, but the bard was gone,
> No more to tune his pipe on plain or hill,
> Nor multiply the moon from Willie's mill.
> But oh! how fondly still that crescent moon
> Hung with her golden horns o'er bonnie Doon,
> As though she look'd to be mis-counted still.

On Mr. Turner's return to Grasby he was no longer able to conduct the services of the Sanctuary, and his place was taken by a curate; still, he continued his visitations to the last, his love for his people being unbounded.

Later, in order that he might be under the care of Dr. Kerr, an old medical friend, he removed to

Cheltenham. There, thirteen years previously, his brother Septimus, as well as his sister-in-law Charlotte, wife of Mr. Horatio Tennyson, had died, and there on April 25th 1879, after much suffering, heroic-ally borne, the summons came to him, and peacefully his spirit passed away

"Across the waters, to the land of rest!"

On his death, Grasby descended to the Laureate, and is now the property of his son, The Hon. Hallam Tennyson. He, as patron, presented to the living his friend, the Rev. J. F. Quirk, for some time curate at Haslemere, who, like his predecessor, is much loved and respected by his people.

Pax in Christo.

Bayons Manor.

"He lean'd not on his fathers but himself."

Hazgrove Manor.

BAYONS MANOR.

In the opening verses of his latest volume of poems, the Laureate thanks Lord Dufferin for the kindness he showed to his son, Mr. Lionel Tennyson, when in India.

In doing so, his grief passes almost beyond control as he pictures to himself the sad scene in the homeward-bound vessel, when near Aden—

> "the coffin fell,
> Fell—and flash'd into the Red Sea,"

yet, remembering that "within our Father's heart the secret lies of this dim world," like a brave man he accepts the situation, merely adding—

> "To question, why
> The sons before the fathers die,
> Not mine!"

This thought, so felicitously expressed, must have been forcibly brought home to the poet three score years before, on the death of his own father,—as his father's father, George Tennyson of Bayons Manor, was then living, hale and hearty, passing "life's late eve" in his beautiful seat, not many miles distant from Somersby.

George Tennyson may in one respect be said to have been the restorer of his family's fortunes. Endowed with great energy and ability he turned his attention in early life to law, and so mastered

> "That codeless myriad of precedent,
> That wilderness of single instances,"

as to beat his way out to wealth and fame.

He was the principal promoter of and subscriber to the magnificent dock at Grimsby, having inherited through his mother's family the valuable Clayton estates in and around the neighbourhood of that town. To these estates he added by purchase those of Bayons Manor and Usselby, whilst his marriage with Miss Turner of Caistor brought him considerable wealth.

Two sons were born to him, the elder, the poet's father, devoting his life to the service of the Church, the younger entering Parliament.

In the year 1825 he lost his wife, and hearing of the poetical tastes of his grandson—though his sympathies with poets were somewhat on a par with Squire Spedding's—he asked him to write an elegy commemorating her death.

The shrewdest sometimes make mistakes, and the learned lawyer with all his sagacity was not an exception to the rule. He had, as Lockhart says of Scott, the zeal of pedigree deeply rooted in him, and was busy at this time tracing his descent from his forbears, and building up the family name. Yet little did he foresee that this slender youth would prove the most illustrious scion of his house, and would cause the name of Tennyson to be known in all lands, for all time, otherwise he would not have passed his celebrated criticism on his grandson's poem, when, putting a half-sovereign into his hands, he damped the lad's aspirations by saying, "There, that is the first money you have ever earned by your poetry, and, take my word for it, it will be the last."

A drive of some twenty miles northward from Somersby, over the wolds of Mid Lincolnshire, and partly along the old Roman road called the High

Street, brings the traveller to a point, where a steep narrow path winds gradually downwards to the rustic village of Tealby. There is an air of deep seclusion

around this old world hamlet, the thatched cottages, and old-fashioned gardens with their high hedgerows, making it such a place as an artist would love, and well entitling it to be called one of the prettiest of the wold villages.

The scenery depicted in the early portion of "Aylmer's Field" might have been taken from this country side, for certainly it is a sleepy land with "little about it stirring save a brook," which, flowing swiftly by, separates the village from the demesne of the d'Eyncourts.

BAYONS MANOR.

On an elevated knoll half hidden among old trees stands Tealby Church, from the porch of which a lovely view is obtained across the wooded valley to Bayons Manor.

In this church Charles Tennyson, after leaving Cambridge, officiated as curate for a short time previous to his becoming vicar of Grasby; and here, according to the Parish Register, the poet's eldest brother, George, who died in infancy, was baptized on 25th May, 1806.

The chancel contains the dust of the poet's grandparents, a short record of their lives being engraved on two brass tablets fixed to the wall over the monument erected to their memory.

BAYONS MANOR.

To the Memory of
George Tennyson, Esquire, of Bayons Manor,
and of Usselby in this County,
Who died 4th July, 1835,
aged 85 years.
He was the son and heir of Michael Tennyson, Esquire, by
Elizabeth, his wife,
Daughter and heiress of George Clayton, Esquire.
He left surviving his two daughters, Elizabeth and Mary,
and his son, the Right Hon. Charles Tennyson, M.P. for Lambeth,
whom he directed by his will to superadd the name of d'Eyncourt
in order to commemorate his descent from
the two ancient families who formerly bore that name and title.
His powerful understanding,
practical wisdom, and sympathising disposition
were a sure resource for all who sought from him
aid or counsel in difficulty or affliction.
Self-denying, but nobly liberal to others,
Constant to his friends, stedfast in his principles,
forgiving, sincere, benevolent, and just,
He commanded the respect and attracted the affection
of all around him.
His remains were attended to the tomb by all classes
from the surrounding county
and deposited by the side of his lamented wife.
Their grateful son prays for the grace
to walk humbly in their steps
and prove his veneration for both his parents
by striving to emulate
their virtues.

To the Memory of
Mary, the wife of George Tennyson, Esquire, of Bayons Manor,
She died on the 20th day of August, 1825,
Aged 72 years.
And her remains are deposited
in the vault beneath this chancel.
She was the daughter of John Turner, Esquire, of Castor, in the county of Lincoln,
by Mary, his wife.
After an union of 50 years she was survived by her husband
who deeply lamented her loss;
and by their own issue,
The Rev. George Clayton Tennyson, LL.D.;
Charles Tennyson, Esquire, representative in Parliament for the burgh of Grimsby;
Elizabeth, the widow of Matthew Russell, Esq., of Brancepeth Castle,
in the county of Durham;
and Mary, the wife of John Bourne, Esquire,
of Dalby, in this county.
By her devoted tenderness as a wife and a mother,
her Constancy, Sincerity, and active benevolence,
by her pure mind, amiable manners, and affectionate disposition,
She was so endeared to her family and the poor.
By them and all who knew her
She was justly respected, loved, and mourned;
and as by her virtues and exemplary life
she practically illustrated the genuine and unobtrusive piety
by which her conduct was uniformly actuated,
so in the hour of death was she resigned and happy,
deriving support through that great trial
from a source which is open to those only
who have lived the life of the righteous.

Descent of Tennyson
from the
Blood Royal of England.

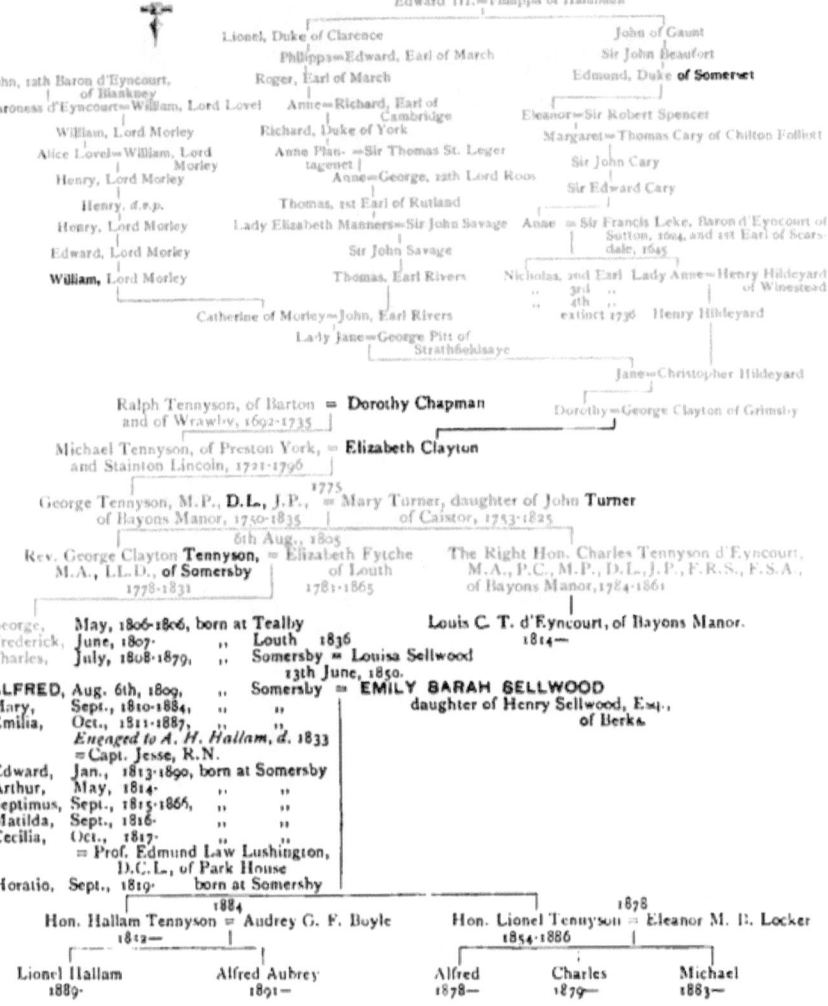

Such tablets assist materially in tracing the pedigree of the Poet Laureate, who, though he smiles "at the claims of long descent" and tells us that "'tis only noble to be good," inherits through his female ancestors some of the noblest blood in England—his lineage extending back to Edward III.

On the death of George Tennyson in 1835 his estates were divided. Those at Great Grimsby passed to his eldest son's family, being now in the possession of the poet's elder brother, Frederick;

while Bayons Manor and the adjoining estates were bequeathed to his younger son, the Right Hon. Charles Tennyson d'Eyncourt.

A tradition prevails that a clause was inserted in the will that the old mansion of Bayons Manor was not to be pulled down, but the author of "Eustace" managed to comply with his father's wishes and still gratify his taste for architecture by erecting the present pile at great cost all round the old house, which is still standing.

It is a common remark among the natives of this part of Lincolnshire that few have any idea of the magnificence of this princely seat, and, even apart from its Tennysonian interest, it well repays a visit. Crossing the little brook and entering the park, the house comes full in view. A moat forms a semi-circle round the front of it, and this is spanned by a drawbridge, passing over which and knocking at the

huge iron-studded gateway of the barbican, entrance is gained to the private grounds, where, on the site of the old garden, Mr. d'Eyncourt, the present owner, frequently played with his cousin, the Laureate in their boyish days.

The exterior of the mansion has every appearance of a mediæval castle. It is built of a hard sandstone found in the neighbourhood, and the colour, being a pleasant brown, gives the structure an appearance of age which its history does not warrant, as its erection is within sixty years.

The interior has been carefully planned and furnished to keep in character with the exterior of the building. The banqueting hall, where, as we read in " Eustace,"

> " Four hundred joyful guests a banquet shared
> In all the form of olden times prepared,"

is a magnificent apartment, resembling the Great Hall at Burleigh House. The library has a large collection of books, and the tapestry room in the tower a connection with literature from the fact that Bulwer Lytton wrote in it "The Last of the Barons." The dining-room contains the family pictures, most noticeable among which is the portrait of the poet's grandfather, George Tennyson, by Sir Thomas Lawrence.

The date of the picture is not known, but from the admirable way in which the head and face are portrayed it evidently is one of the earlier and finer works of this great artist. Charles Tennyson wrote a sonnet on the death of Lawrence, and, gazing on this beautiful portrait, we feel how true and forcible are his lines—

> "What hand, but his, so excellently knew
> The shadow of our lineaments?
>
> .   .   .   .   .
>
> Age smiled, portray'd in all its sober calm,
> Unvext, of grandsire aspect, pale and meek."

There is no portrait of the Laureate now at Bayons Manor, as Admiral Tennyson d'Eyncourt removed it some years ago to his London residence, but in the dining-room there is another very interesting portrait —that of the poet's uncle—to whom Tennyson refers as "my father's brother" in his dedication of "Harold."

This is the Right Hon. Charles Tennyson d'Eyncourt, who, after graduating at Cambridge, entered Parliament and for many years was a prominent member of the House of Commons, representing successively Grimsby, Bletchingley, Stamford, and Lambeth. A man of very cultured tastes, had his time not

GEORGE TENNYSON.
From a Painting by Sr. Thomas Lawrence, P.R.A.

been so fully occupied with politics, he too "might have won the Poet's name," as the elegy he wrote commemorating the death in 1842 of his son, Captain Eustace Tennyson d'Eyncourt, who fell a victim to yellow fever at Barbadoes, within a few days after his arrival from England to join his regiment, shows considerable poetical talent, one of the couplets being specially noteworthy—

"Maintain the people's rights. The Queen defend.
Obey the laws. To God your soul commend."

Statesman, scholar, and poet, at a ripe age, in 1861, he was gathered to his fathers, and buried in Tealby Church, being succeeded in his estates by his eldest son, George Hildeyard Tennyson d'Eyncourt, registrar of the most distinguished Order of St. Michael and St. George.

On the death of this gentleman in 1871 the estates passed to his brother, Admiral Edwin Clayton Tennyson d'Eyncourt, C.B., a naval officer who has served with distinction in China and in the Gulf of Finland during the Crimean War.

By a family arrangement Bayons Manor is now the property of the youngest surviving son of the poet's uncle, Louis Charles Tennyson d'Eyncourt, Esq., a gentleman widely known from his long and honourable tenure of the office of Senior Metropolitan Magistrate.

In 1890, to the regret of all, he tendered his resignation to the Home Secretary, carrying with him in his retirement the love and esteem of troops of friends, which his kindness and courtesy had gained for him.

The Grange and the Mill.

"I loved the brimming wave that swam
Thro' quiet meadows round the mill,"

Somersby Grange

THE GRANGE AND THE MILL.

ONE of the chief characteristics of Tennyson is his retiring nature. All his days he has dwelt very much apart from men, loving "the life removed"— the life, perhaps, best suited to develop the extraordinary gifts he has been endowed with. No one is more apt to be idolized than a popular poet, and, in consequence, snares and pitfalls beset his path, which, if he fall into, will dim the fire of his genius, if not altogether extinguish it. Burns' visit to Edinburgh proved a downward step in his career. Society in the *salons* of London was a Will-o'-the-Wisp to Byron; and the muse of the genial Sir Walter, may be said to have left him when he exchanged the quiet retirement of Ashestiel for the splendours of Abbotsford.

Whether or not warned by the mistakes of his predecessors, Tennyson, at an early age, when his name began to be mooted in literary circles as the rising poet of his generation, withdrew from the world.

You will not find him, as Howitt says, at the dinner tables of the great, or in the crowded drawing-rooms of London, only his voice is heard—the man never to be seen. "He is gone down into his garden, to his beds of spices, to feed in his garden, and gather lilies." "He is wandering in some dreamland, beneath the shade of old and charmed forests, by far off shores, where

"all night
The plunging seas draw backward from the land
Their moon-led waters white":

by the old mill-dam, thinking of the merry miller and his pretty daughter; or is wandering over the open wolds, where

"Norland whirlwinds blow."

From all these places; from the silent corridor of an ancient convent; from the drear monotony of "the moated grange," or the ferny forest beneath "the talking oak," comes the voice of Tennyson, rich, dreamy, passionate, yet not impatient, . whispering into the ear a startling word of counsel or moving one to deeds of mercy."

The drear monotony of the moated grange, and the merry miller and his pretty daughter were among the earliest themes of the poet's muse.

It was when a student at Cambridge that he first came before the world as a poet, prefixing his name

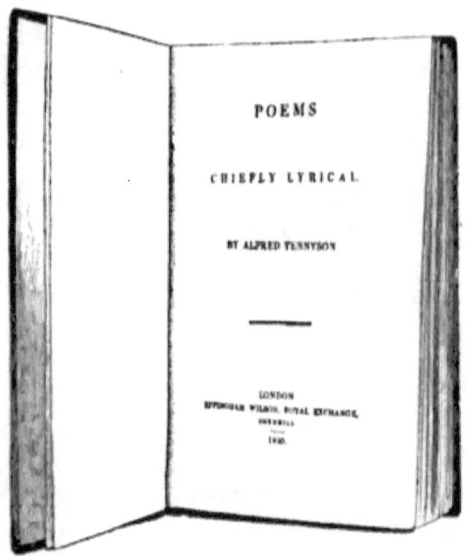

to a thin volume, entitled "Poems Chiefly Lyrical." Many of these, in the late editions, have been wholly suppressed, others considerably altered, but in this rare duodecimo is to be found a poem, "Mariana," which is so perfect in what Kingsley aptly calls "tone" that even the critical hand of the Laureate has not seen fit to change scarcely one word since first it came forth, fresh from his pen.

In this poem Tennyson's object is to present a picture of weariness and dreariness; and taking for his subject a woman abandoned to lonely misery, he so handles the details of the landscape as to make them tell of long years of protracted wretchedness and hopeless suffering. We are not told whether death or desertion has caused the lamp of her life to burn so dimly; all we know is that "he cometh not"; and so those things which before tended to make life joyous and happy are left unloved and unheeded; neglect takes the place of care, and all goes rotting to decay. Black moss grows in the flower plots, the nails are rusted, the sheds broken, the latch clinks, the thatch is weedy and worn. When the day is at its brightest she is unable to perceive it, as her eyes are dim with tears. Night comes; surely sleep will steep her brows "in slumber's holy balm"; but no, even

"In sleep she seem'd to walk forlorn,
Till cold winds woke the gray-eyed morn
About the lonely moated grange."

Thus her life is passed in hoping, loving, remembering, waiting—waiting, remembering, loving, hoping—till at last she vanishes from our sight, crying

"I am aweary, aweary,
Oh God, that I were dead!"

Though "Mariana" is founded on that stray thought in Shakespeare's "Measure for Measure,"—

"there, at the moated grange, resides this dejected Mariana,"—

it is far more due to Tennyson than to the Bard of Avon that her fame has spread through the world.

The poem, in fact, may be said to be indissolubly associated with the Laureate's name, and is one which all his critics delight in praising.

Thus we find Fitzgerald, after purchasing a copy of "Poems Chiefly Lyrical," writing to his friend Allen, "I have bought A. Tennyson's poems. How good Mariana is!" And evidently it was the same poem that Carlyle always associated with the name of his illustrious contemporary, for when asked by Emerson to write him a description of Tennyson, he says—"Alfred, you see in his verses, is a native of moated granges."

It is doubtful what was the original signification of the word grange, but prior to the Reformation it denoted the farm buildings attached to a monastery, where the grain paid as tithes was stored; in later times coming to be used simply to designate a yeoman's dwelling—a house immediately inferior to a hall.

When situated in lonely districts such granges were often surrounded by a deep fosse or ditch, which, when filled with water, gave to the inmates a certain sense of security. Moated granges of this description still exist in the fenny districts of Lincolnshire, but they are many miles distant from Somersby, hence the scenery which colours this poem is not taken from the country round the poet's birthplace, as it has no features in common with the landscape depicted in "Mariana."

With these low-lying districts, however, the poet was quite familiar, especially with "the waste enormous marsh," that wide tract of fertile land which has grown above the sea and stretches from the wolds to the coast-line, crossed by the family when journeying

from Somersby to Mablethorpe, one of the watering-
places they used to visit.

Three or four miles before we reach Mablethorpe
the road passes through a very bleak piece of country,
where, owing to the winds that sweep inward from
the sea, scarcely a tree or shrub relieves the mono-
tony of the scene. Here in the vicinity of Maltby-
le-marsh the Misses Tennyson, driving along in their

father's
coach, were wont
to call a dreary red brick house, which stood a
little way off the road in a rather low flat with a
very few trees about it, "the moated grange"; and
thus they may be said to have been the first to

endeavour to localize Mariana's abode. In this respect they have had many imitators, for how often, on seeing some old deserted house, has the thought suggested itself to the mind of others, surely this must be the moated grange of Tennyson!

To take a case in point; "I passed the summer months this year," says a writer, "in a village of Brabant, that nestles on the skirts of the old Forêt de Soignies. Strolling one evening down a little valley by a path that was new to me, I came suddenly on 'Mariana's' moated grange. That and no other, verily — an old, abandoned manor-house, bristling with gables, its walls moss-coated, its moat covered with green scum; its garden wild, weedy, and dank, and beyond the edges of it a marsh fringed with poplars. Could the poet have beheld this strange picture ere he created his poem? or was the resemblance purely fortuitous? As I eyed the place, wondering at its weirdness, and fancying that in some upper chamber Mariana must be lying dead, or I should hear her moan, a white mist gathered on the face of the marsh, gathered and crept and crawled and circled me waist high, and then swallowed me up, me and the moated grange and the poplar spires—oozing, eddying, swirling, till nothing was left."

It would be easy to quote similar experiences from the writings of others, but it is needless to do so, as it is impossible to identify this or that place as the moated grange, for though certain outward objects no doubt suggested certain ideas to the poet, he here draws largely on his fancy's resources, fusing together imaginatively into one picture several different visual experiences; as Shelley writes—

> "He will watch from dawn to gloom
> The lake-reflected sun illume
> The yellow bees in the ivy-bloom,
> Nor heed nor see what things they be;
> But from these, create he can
> Forms more real than real man,—
> Nurslings of immortality."

In the vicinity of Somersby, adjoining the manor-house (painfully close to it, as one has remarked), stands a gaunt, castellated building, which has often excited the wonder of those who have visited the district, quite a little storm of controversy raging round its old lichen-covered walls.

For one thing, its name seems doubtful, as it has

many aliases—being known as Somersby Grange, Somersby Old Hall, Somersby Farm, etc., etc.

The same dubiety also exists as to whether or not the poet makes any allusion to it in his poems, many fancying that from the air of gloom which surrounds it, it is just such a place as might be associated with the idea of the moated grange; while others, taking into account the fact that it was once tenanted by a certain John Baumber, a noted Lincolnshire agriculturist, have set it down as the typical residence of the "Northern Farmer."

Of the history of this old house there is little to record, save that Sir J. Vanbrugh is credited with having been its architect. Built entirely of bricks, externally it has rather an imposing appearance, but, inside, the wainscoted rooms are small, and not fitted for the requirements of modern life.

It is a pleasant variety to turn one's steps from this dreary building, and wending our way through the gently sloping meadows to the little brook, follow its windings for a mile or so, until it is dammed up to turn the mill of Stockworth.

Pinkworth Mill.

If the melancholy which broods round Somersby Grange has a tendency to depress one's spirits, the sweetness of this rural spot will cause them not only to regain their equilibrium, but to rebound in the opposite direction, and we feel this in almost every line of the poet when he writes of similar scenery.

Of all the earlier poems of Tennyson, there was none which added more to his growing reputation than "The Miller's Daughter," its homely beauty and glimpses of domestic happiness captivating at once the imagination of the public. Our Queen was so much touched by its simple strains, that when death removed the Laureate's crown

"from the brows
Of him that utter'd nothing base,"

it was the recollection of this bucolic idyll which decided Her Majesty, in face of all opposition, to confer the much coveted wreath on its author.

A poet in the first instance, Tennyson is also a great moral teacher. His poems have always an aim for good; the lessons are there, if we would only read them. He selects some character, tells a story in language all his own, and leaves the reader to draw his conclusions.

The marriage relationship is a favourite theme with him, and many of his finest poems circle round it. In "The Lord of Burleigh," "Lady Clare," etc., he brushes aside all traditions, and with exquisite pathos, revels in that true sentiment he is so fond of, showing that when there exists between two persons what Scott calls "the secret sympathy," their union is almost sure to be a happy one. But again in "Maud" and "Locksley Hall" he declaims in tones of thunder against those who sin against "the truth of love," and especially in "Aylmer's Field," taking for his text the words, "Behold, your house is left unto you desolate!", he teaches the lesson of pride trampling on love, and leaving in its train desolation and ruin.

In "The Miller's Daughter" there is a beautiful contrast to all this, for here

"Love took up the harp of Life, and smote on all the chords
    with might;
  Smote the chord of Self, that, trembling, pass'd in music out
    of sight."

THE GRANGE AND THE MILL.

The squire, when little more than a boy, falls in love with the pretty daughter of a wealthy miller. There are no hindrances to the match. His father being dead, he has inherited his fortune, and is now his own lord and master; only his mother has to be won round, and she, like most fond mothers, dotes on her son, and soon yields her consent :—

> "She wish'd me happy, but she thought
> I might have look'd a little higher."

So he is wedded in the springtime of life, when everything has a bright roseate hue, and though some might expect that after his honeymoon was over, this young fellow would change like leaves in autumn, and begin to think he might have married better, it is not so; but on the contrary, his life with his first love is like one long summer's day, when the sun shines out in all its brightness, and with the approaching sunset only one cloud appears on the horizon—the thought that soon death must separate them from one another.

> "Yet fill my glass: give me one kiss:
> My own sweet Alice, we must die.
> There's somewhat in this world amiss
> Shall be unriddled by and by.

>   There's somewhat flows to us in life,
>   But more is taken quite away.
>   Pray, Alice, pray, my darling wife,
>   That we may die the self-same day."

As has been said, this lyric was one of the earliest that Tennyson wrote, appearing in his second volume of poems published about the close of 1832.

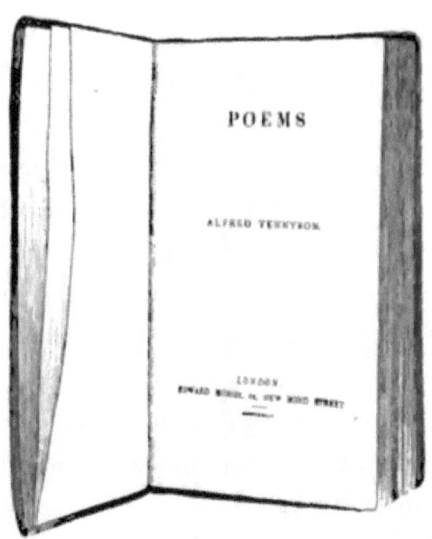

In the spring of that year, Hallam visited the poet at Somersby, where Tennyson had been residing more or less since the death of his father, and in an interesting letter to Trench he throws some light on the poems then in manuscript.

(Postmark) Spilsby.

"March 20, 1832.

"Alfred I was most glad to find better than I had apprehended. I see no ground for thinking he has anything really serious to ail him. His mind is what it always was, or rather brighter, and more vigorous. I regret, with you, that you have never had the opportunity of knowing more of him. His nervous temperament and habits of solitude give an appearance of affectation to his manner, which is no true interpreter of the man, and wears off on further knowledge. . . . . I have persuaded him, I think, to publish without further delay. There is written the amount of a volume rather larger than the former, and certainly, unless the usual illusion of manuscript deceives me, more free from blemishes and more masterly in power."

Probably "The Miller's Daughter" was written at Cambridge, as the mill is said to be taken from Trumpington Mill near that city, but there are several touches in the poem, such as the references to "the wolds" and "the white chalk-quarry," which seem to indicate that, consciously or unconsciously, the haunts of his boyhood were present to the poet's mind, wherever he wrote it.

The little stream which runs along the happy valley of Somersby turns the wheels of no less than three mills, and in the poet's youthful days it supplied a fourth with water. This last was almost within a stone's cast of his father's rectory, and here the poet when a child would watch

> "The sleepy pool above the dam,
> The pool beneath it never still."

This mill has long ago disappeared, and the nearest to Somersby is now that called Stockworth, in the parish of Hagworthingham. As the distance does not exceed two miles, it is not beyond the limits of conjecture, knowing as we do that the poet's favourite walk was by the banks of the brook, to imagine that in some of those afternoon strolls, so beautifully described in "In Memoriam," he and his friend would often turn their steps hitherward, especially as it is one of the sweetest spots in all the surrounding country.

The mill and most of the land in its vicinity are owned by the Ingilbys, an ancient family whose seat, "the old manorial hall" of Harrington being the nearest residence to Somersby—must have been one of those landmarks familiar to the poet in his youth.

The hall, built of red brick, is a fine specimen of a Jacobean mansion, and dates from 1681, having probably been erected on the site of an older structure.

Within its policies stands the Church of Harrington, rebuilt about five-and-thirty years ago, which contains, besides other relics of the past, the effigy of a knight in chain armour, with legs crossed and feet resting on a hound, conjuring to memory the warrior "fore-father" of Locksley Hall.

96 THE GRANGE AND THE MILL.

Another beautiful Lincolnshire seat which, though distant a few miles from Somersby, might still be said to be within the boundaries of the Laureate's

country, is Scrivelsby Court, the home of the Dymokes, who, as lineal descendants of the Marmions, have for centuries been hereditary Grand Champions of England.

The Marmions were a Norman family which came over to England at the Conquest, and to them William the Conqueror assigned, with other lands, the manor of Scrivelsby, on condition of their filling the office of King's Champion.

Scott revived the memory of the family by the hero

of his rhymed romance, but his

> "Lord of Fontenaye,
> Of Lutterward, and Scrivelbaye,"

was a purely fictitious character as, two centuries previous to the battle of Flodden, the family became extinct owing to the death of Philip de Marmion in 1292.

The Court and Championship then passed by marriage to the Dymokes, and from the time of Richard II. it was the custom for the head of this family, at the coronation of the English monarchs, to ride into Westminster Hall clad in bright armour, and throwing down the gauntlet, to challenge all who gainsayed the Sovereign's title to the crown.

But 'the old order changeth, yielding place to new.' The day on which the Laureate, adorned with blue ribbons, walked down the streets of Louth in procession with his schoolfellows in honour of the coronation of George the Fourth, witnessed the enactment for the last time of this remnant of feudalism, as on the accession of William the Fourth the ceremony was allowed to fall into abeyance and not renewed afterwards.

98   THE GRANGE AND THE MILL.

Scrivelsby, from its associations with chivalry, and from the Tennysons being allied to the Marmions, through their descent from Sir Edward Hilary, son of Joane de Marmion, must doubtless have had a special interest for the poet.

Partly girt with a moat, the Court is situated in a magnificent park—the entrance to which has been guarded for the last four hundred years by a crowned lion.

"HERE THE LION-GUARDED GATE."

Burleigh House.

"A mansion more majestic
Than all those she saw before."

Burleigh House.

BURLEIGH HOUSE.

AFTER the publication of the volume containing "The Miller's Daughter" Tennyson remained silent for many years. His college acquaintances, with keener insight than their contemporaries, had warmly applauded his verses, but the all-powerful reviewers of the day, in the persons of Christopher North and Lockhart, were not so encouraging. Henceforth the poet determined to fulfil the expectations of his friends by winning the approval of his detractors, in other words, to perfect himself in his art.

It took him ten years to do so. Right noble was his self-control, for to work and wait thus must have been no easy task for one who knew that powers had been entrusted to him far in excess of his fellows. But the poet by his long self-discipline showed that genius is sometimes amenable to control, and the reception accorded by all to the next edition of his poems, published in 1842, proved the truth of his own maxim that

> " Self-reverence, self-knowledge, self-control,
> These three alone lead life to sovereign power."

In this celebrated edition are several of Tennyson's masterpieces. The quantity is not great, but the quality is of the finest. Every sort of metre is tried, every kind of subject handled; in short, it seems to have been the poet's desire to satisfy the most diverse tastes.

Mrs. Carlyle, with her love for metaphysics, is captivated by " The Vision of Sin," while her husband's heart is stirred by the spirit of energy breathing forth from " Ulysses."

Dickens takes the volumes with him to the seaside, and in rapture exclaims, " What a great creature Tennyson is!" Even Wordsworth acknowledges his superiority to himself in a letter to a friend, calling him " the first of our living poets."

While he thus won the approval of his comrades in the domain of literature, not less enthusiastic in his praise was the great mass of the poetry-reading public. The country rang with the fervid music of "Locksley Hall"; as one has said, "another King Alfred was crowned in England."

For the most part the poems are not founded on fact, but spring from the luxuriance of the poet's imagination. Some, like "Godiva" and "Morte d'Arthur," are idealized reminiscences of old legends; others, pure idylls — what Ruskin would call the hearth-side poetry of domestic life. There is, however, one poem in this notable collection, that ballad of ballads, "The Lord of Burleigh," which is more than the creation of a poet's fancy, being rather a narrative in verse, with the usual poetic licenses, of the wooing and romantic marriage of the tenth Earl and first Marquis of Exeter.

From one of Fitzgerald's letters we get a glimpse of Tennyson on a visit to Mirehouse, in the Cumberland hills, during the spring of 1835, in which we are told of Spedding sitting up with the poet "conning over the 'Morte d'Arthur,' 'Lord of Burleigh,'" etc., etc. This is the first record we have of the poem, but from the proximity of Burleigh House to Lincolnshire, and the great influence of the Exeter family in that county, the incidents round which the poem hinges must have been familiar to Tennyson from a very early period of his life.

As the story goes, near the close of last century Henry Cecil, heir to his uncle the Earl of Exeter,

secretly left his home, and, crossing England, took up his quarters in the hostelry of Bolas, a rural village situated amid rolling slopes of corn in the heart of Shropshire. In order to escape recognition Mr. Cecil had adopted a peculiar cut of wig, but

"his Lord Burleigh look, serene and serious,
A something of imposing and mysterious,"

BURLEIGH HOUSE.   105

roused the suspicions of the landlord, and he was requested to leave. In his extremity he betook himself to a farm hard by the church, tenanted by a Mr. Hoggins, and finding in this quiet house a lodging suitable to his taste he resided there for two years.

To one who had seen so much of high life in his youth, the humdrum routine of an ordinary farm-house must have grown rather monotonous had not "love possess'd the atmosphere," the farmer's

daughter captivating by her naïve simplicity and gentleness, the heart of the stranger. She was a maid of fifteen summers when Mr. Jones—for he had adopted that *alias*—came to reside with her father, and being still at school he interested himself in her education by becoming her tutor—in this and other ways winning her affection.

"When two love well, events must onward move."

Banns of Marriage between _____

Nº 54 *John Jones* of *this* Parish _____ and *Sarah Hoggins* of *this* Parish _____ were Married in this *Church* by *Licence* this *thirteenth* Day of *April* in the Year One Thousand Seven Hundred and *ninety* by me *Cresswell Tayleur*
This Marriage was solemnized between Us { *John Jones* / *Sarah Hoggins* }
In the Presence of *John Pigeon* / *Sarah Adams*

On April 13th, 1790, they were married in the quaint little church of Bolas, the courtship and ceremony being thus described by Tennyson in three of his most felicitous verses.

"In her ear he whispers gaily,
  'If my heart by signs can tell,
Maiden, I have watch'd thee daily,
  And I think thou lov'st me well.'

"She replies, in accents fainter,
  'There is none I love like thee.'
He is but a landscape-painter,
  And a village maiden she.

"He to lips, that fondly falter,
  Presses his without reproof:
Leads her to the village altar,
  And they leave her father's roof."

Mr. Cecil preserved his incognito. Without acquainting his wife of his prospects, he quietly settled

down in a house which he had built half a mile from the village, giving it the name of Bolas Villa, now changed to Burleigh, and considerably altered by the present proprietor.

Three years of married life had passed here, a girl and a boy being born to them (the latter of whom died in infancy), when in 1793 the demise of his uncle, Lord Exeter, obliged Mr. Cecil to throw off his disguise.

Not knowing very well how to break the news to his wife, he merely told her that he was called on business to Lincolnshire, and that he would like her to accompany him. To this she willingly agreed, and accordingly, mounted on a pillion behind her husband, they set out from Bolas *en route* for Stamford.

Travelling was by no means easy then, and what now could be accomplished in a certain number of hours occupied at that time as many days, if not weeks. It had, however, its advantages, for in the different stages of the journey it allowed them ample time to see some of the great mansions of England near which they happened to pass.

The Earl must have found it hard to keep his secret, for at these houses, greatly to his wife's surprise, they met with the most cordial reception, yet so confiding was her nature she did not trouble him with questions, and the grandeur, far from making her envious, rather deepened the love she bore her husband.

> "All he shows her makes him dearer:
> Evermore she seems to gaze
> On that cottage growing nearer,
> Where they twain will spend their days."

Thus happily they rode by easy stages through Cannock Chase, Lichfield, and Leicester, until at

length the spires of Stamford came in view. They did not stop in the town, but riding through its quaint old streets to the southern boundary, soon reached the gates of the avenue leading up to the ancestral seat of the Cecils. The crisis was now at hand; the truth had to be told; no longer could her rank be hidden, and her feelings may be imagined when, on expressing her admiration at the magnificence and incomparable beauty of the mansion, she heard her husband say—

"All of this is mine and thine."

"It was a sensation worth dying for, says Hazlitt. The world we live in was worth making, had it been only for this. *Ye Thousand and One Tales of the Arabian Nights' Entertainments!* hide your diminished heads! I never wish to have been a lord, but when I think of this story."

The Lord of Burleigh had no reason to regret the choice he had made in his Countess, for her simple manners and kindly ways gained for her the love of all classes, from Queen Charlotte down to the humblest of the Earl's numerous dependents.

But the duties involved by her rank pressed heavily upon her, and though her cares were brightened by the birth of a son (the father of the present Marquis of Exeter) and the untiring devotion of her husband, three years after her happy home-coming had scarcely elapsed, when Death severed the white bonds which Love had woven.

"At Burleigh House, near Stamford," ran the obituary, January, 1797, "aged 24, to the inexpressible surprise and concern of all acquainted with her, the Right Hon. Countess of Exeter."

> "Weeping, weeping late and early,
>   Walking up and pacing down,
> Deeply mourn'd the Lord of Burleigh,
>   Burleigh-house by Stamford-town."

Burleigh House, or, as it is sometimes designated, Burghley, is situated really in Northamptonshire, on the borders of the counties of Rutland and Lincoln. It was erected between the years 1575 and 1587 by Sir William Cecil, Lord High Treasurer of England and confidential adviser of his Sovereign Queen Elizabeth.

John Thorpe was the architect, and in drawing the plans he departed from the old lines, and introduced into England a style of architecture partly borrowed from Italy, partly created by his own lively imagination. The change, like every other change, was viewed with considerable apprehension by Conservatives of the time, one of whom characterized the style as "curious to the eie, *like paper worke*, than substantiall for continuance." In spite however of such gloomy forebodings the house has withstood the storms of three centuries, and to-day looks so fresh, that one might fancy it had been erected in the Victorian era rather than in "the spacious times of great Elizabeth."

In the olden days it was perhaps better known than it is now, as the mail coaches on the great North Road ran past the lodge gates, and the mansion being one of the show houses of England, and by the kind permission of its owners open to the public, travellers often availed themselves of the stoppage at Stamford to visit it.

An interesting entry in Sir Walter Scott's journal records a visit he paid to Burleigh when journeying to London in 1826.

"It is long since," he writes, "I travelled this road, having come up to town chiefly by sea of late years. . . . Visited Burleigh this morning; the first time I ever saw that grand place, where there are so many objects of interest and curiosity. The house is magnificent, in the style of James I.'s reign, and consequently in mixed Gothic. Of paintings I know nothing; so shall attempt to say nothing. But whether to connoisseurs, or to an ignorant admirer like myself, the Salvator Mundi, by Carlo Dolci, must seem worth a king's ransom."

The picture here alluded to of the Saviour blessing the elements hangs in the jewel closet at Burleigh House, and is considered the gem of the collection, but it is not a little strange that Sir Walter, who devoured all that was romantic, makes no reference to the extremely interesting picture of Henry, tenth Earl and first Marquis of Exeter, Sarah, his Countess, and their daughter, Lady Sophia Cecil, which occupies the place of honour in the great billiard-room.

This exquisitely painted family piece was finished by Sir Thomas Lawrence in the year in which the Countess died. The Marquis, a man of noble bearing, stands by the side of his wife, his left arm thrown lovingly round her shoulder. With wide blue eyes the Countess gazes wistfully out of the picture, her face being so singularly pure and beautiful that it is not difficult to realize how Mr. Cecil fell in love with her and grieved so bitterly at her untimely end.

In her arms she clasps her daughter, Lady Sophia Cecil, a bright laughing girl of tender years.

This young lady became the wife of the Right Hon. Henry Manvers Pierrepont of Conholt-Park, and through the marriage of her only child with Lord Charles Wellesley, the present Duke of Wellington is a great-grandson of the heroine of Tennyson's ballad, "The Lord of Burleigh."

In Memoriam.

" 'Tis better to have loved and lost
Than never to have loved at all."

Arthur H. Hallam.

IN MEMORIAM.

IN his address to James Spedding, who was mourning the loss of a brother, Tennyson, in trying to comfort his friend, touches upon the mysterious ways of the Almighty.

>'Tis strange that those we lean on most,
>   Those in whose laps our limbs are nursed,
>   Fall into shadow, soonest lost :
>Those we love first are taken first.
>
>God gives us love. Something to love
>   He lends us ; but, when love is grown
>   To ripeness, that on which it throve
>Falls off, and love is left alone.

Little did the poet think when he wrote these lines that they would prove only too true in his own case, and that he, whom he leaned on most—Arthur Henry Hallam—would be taken from him not many months afterwards.

It was at Trinity College, Cambridge, that Tennyson and Hallam first met each other, both having matriculated there in the autumn of 1828; and as like draws to like, an intimacy naturally sprang up between these two men of genius, ripening with growing years. Unlike Hallam, the poet did not reside within the precincts of the college, but had his rooms first in the Rose Crescent and afterwards

at No. 55 Corpus Buildings, the last house in a terrace so called from its proximity to Corpus Christi College.

Situated in the central and pleasant part of the town, the view from his windows must at that time have embraced the great quadrangle of King's College flanked by its still greater chapel, from which

might be heard on a still evening the throbbing tones of the "high-built" organ.

Of the seventeen colleges of Cambridge, Trinity, King's, and St. John's occupy the foremost place, not only in point of scholarship and learning, but also in beauty of situation. Closely adjoining one another, their halls and quadrangles, cloisters and chapels, fountains and beautiful pleasure grounds

through which under many a bridge the river Cam glides quietly, form as pleasant a retreat for the pursuit of knowledge as is to be found all the world over.

The scenery at the back of these colleges passes vividly before the eye when one reads Tennyson's lines recounting a visit he paid to the old rooms of his friend.

> I past beside the reverend walls
> In which of old I wore the gown;
> I roved at random thro' the town,
> And saw the tumult of the halls;

And heard once more in college fanes
　　The storm their high-built organs make,
　　And thunder-music, rolling, shake
The prophet blazon'd on the panes ;

And caught once more the distant shout,
　　The measured pulse of racing oars
　　Among the willows ; paced the shores
And many a bridge, and all about

The same gray flats again, and felt
　　The same, but not the same ; and last
　　Up that long walk of limes I past
To see the rooms in which he dwelt.

The contemporaries of **Tennyson at Cambridge** could not complain, as the poet Gray did a hundred years before when a student at Peterhouse, that their undergraduate life was for dulness to be compared to the lot of a blind horse going round and round in a mill. On the contrary, these years were "dawn-golden times," years which Henry Lushington used to look back upon as the happiest in his life, "the days, the nights being smoked away in free gladness, in laughter and uninterrupted talk."

Leaving out of account the many sports and pastimes—such as balloon ascents, amateur theatricals, boat-racing on the Cam—which, hardly known before, then first came into vogue—the intellectual activity which prevailed during this time at Cambridge may be said to have reached high water mark.

Never before had "that long walk of limes" been paced by so many talented youths as were now to be found traversing its "ambrosial aisles," for among them might have been seen Tennyson and Thackeray, Hallam and Lushington, Spedding and Milnes, Trench and Alford, Kinglake, Kemble, Thompson, Brookfield, Merivale, Venables,—men who did so much in later life to mould the literature of the century.

It is little cause for wonder then, that poetry, the highest expression of intellectual thought, should have filled the very air, and that of all the prizes in the gift of the University none was more eagerly coveted than the Chancellor's medal for English verse. The competition was open to all students of the several colleges, and many entered the ranks hoping for the prize.

Milnes, writing to his father, informed him that his poem on Timbuctoo was now finished, and he buoyed himself with hopes of success, as his verses were liked by his own set, which was a good sign.

With no less zeal Hallam, who had already made a name for himself at Eton by the splendid verses he had contributed to the *Eton Miscellany*, joined in the contest, writing his poem (as he told Gladstone, then an undergraduate at Oxford), 'in a sovereign vein of poetic scorn for anybody's opinion who did not value Plato and Milton.'

Tennyson was one of the few who concerned himself little about the matter, and it is questionable if he would have competed for the medal at all had not his father strongly advised him to do so. Accordingly he resuscitated an old poem which he had written some years before on the Battle of Armageddon, and, having altered it a little, sent it in for the theme of Timbuctoo.

How delighted Dr. Tennyson must have been when the news reached him at Somersby of the burst of applause with which his son's poem was greeted at Cambridge; for not only did it secure for its author the much coveted medal, but it caused quite a sensation in literary circles, winning the attraction of such men as Landor and many others, who were of opinion that in imaginative power nothing had been written equal to it since Milton.

Nor were those, who, like Kemble, believed that in Tennyson's mind was heaped in abundance material for the very greatest works—of which "Timbuctoo" was only the first faint dawn—disappointed in the estimate they had formed of his powers when, in 1830, "Poems Chiefly Lyrical," made its appearance. With its publication the poet's fame and position, as far as Cambridge was concerned, were secure; for, just as at Somersby, his brothers and sisters had always deferred to him in literary matters, so here in this wider sphere he was almost idolized by his companions—so much so that Trench had to sound a note of warning in case his friends might materially injure him.

The highest honours they had it in their power to bestow had already been conferred upon him, as shortly before this time the poet, along with Hallam, had been elected a member of that exclusive body entitled the Cambridge Conversazione Society.

This club had now been in existence for about ten years, having become famous in the time of Sterling, Buller, and Maurice. Owing to the numbers being limited to twelve, vacancies were extremely rare, the greatest care being bestowed on the election of new members. The Apostles—for so they were named in derision—no doubt by envious aspirants to membership—lived in the closest intimacy, meeting usually once a week in each other's rooms, there to hold debate

> on mind and art,
> And labour, and the changing mart,
> And all the framework of the land.

Though the society originated in St. John's College,

the meetings were transferred to Trinity, being often held in Hallam's rooms, which were situated on the

central staircase of the south side of the New Court. At such gatherings the poet was often present, but his making a speech or taking any part in the debates was a thing unknown, being in this respect a striking contrast to his friend, who was considered the orator of the society.

> And last the master-bowman, he,
>   Would cleave the mark. A willing ear
>   We lent him. Who, but hung to hear
> The rapt oration flowing free.

Oratory was only one of the many gifts Hallam

possessed, his knowledge on all subjects being hardly credible of one at his age, as he seemed to turn the rays of a flaming torch on everything he handled. No philosophical question, however abstruse, was beyond his powers of mastery; while his reading was so wide as to embrace not only the whole range of English literature, but that of Foreign literature as well.

Add to these mental qualities the most tender and gentle disposition, a reverence for all that was good, a pure and blameless character,

"The graceful tact, the Christian art,"

and it is easy to understand how the poet was attracted to him and made him his bosom friend. The confidence thus reposed was not misplaced, for Hallam looked up to Tennyson, as possessing a much more lofty intellect than his own, in his letters never tiring to predict the heights the poet would attain to. "I hope you will buy and read Alfred Tennyson's poems," he wrote Mr. Gladstone, June 30, 1830, "I am sure you will perceive their extraordinary merit," and again, "I consider Tennyson as promising fair to be the greatest poet of our generation, perhaps of our century."

The poet did not return to Cambridge after the death of his father in 1831, but Hallam remained at Trinity till January, 1832, when he took his degree. The companionship was thus for a short time broken, but the intimacy was soon renewed, as we find him in the spring of that year "a welcome guest" at Somersby.

"I am now at Somersby," he writes Trench, "not only as the friend of Alfred Tennyson, but as the lover of his sister. An attachment on my part of near two years' standing, and a mutual engagement of one year, are, I fervently hope, only the commencement of an union which circumstances may not impair and the grave itself not conclude."

On his return to London, Hallam, at the earnest wish of his father, occupied himself with the study of law, throwing all his energies into it,—in his own words, "slaving at the outworks of my profession." His health, which had always been a source of anxiety to his friends, now began apparently to improve, and his spirits, which before had been liable to sudden fits of depression, became uniformly gay.

In the autumn of 1833, requiring rest and change after an attack of influenza, he accompanied his father on a visit to Germany, and prolonging his travels into Austrian territory, reached the capital of that country.

On the afternoon of the 15th September, being somewhat fatigued with previous exertions, he lay down to rest on a sofa while his father went out to take a walk in the streets of Vienna. On returning, the historian, fancying Arthur was sleeping, sat down to his letters, and became so engrossed in writing that he forgot his son's presence until struck with his stillness and silence, it suddenly flashed across his mind that something was wrong. Alas! his worst fears were verified; in the interval, without premonitory symptoms of any kind, a sudden rush of blood to the head had terminated his son's life.

So went this sweet and beautiful soul "thro' the strait and dreadful pass of death," yet to him this sudden call was great gain, for "he was on his way to God and could rest in nothing short of Him."

News in these days took a long time to travel; but at length it fell with awful suddenness on his friends at home, extracts from some of the letters which passed between his college companions showing how grievously they felt the loss they had sustained in his death.

"I did not think to have written to you so soon," (wrote Trench to Donne, October 9th, 1833,) "and very much would have rejoiced if I had no need to do so; but it is, I am sure, better that you should know the great and common loss we have sustained, and indeed our whole generation. Our dear and delightful friend, Arthur Hallam, who had for some time been travelling in Germany, has not been permitted to return. The fatal event took place at Vienna; the immediate cause, as you may have anticipated, pressure of blood upon the brain. His father was with him. I have not been able to learn any particulars, but fear that there can be now no doubt of the truth of the intelligence, having heard it from two quarters. . . . I am sure we must all feel very deeply for his family, and especially for poor Miss Tennyson. We must give them what we have, which are our prayers, that their hearts may be comforted, and that she may find rest and consolation in Him Who can alone give it."

It would be difficult to describe the grief at Somersby when the sad tidings of Hallam's death reached the family there. "When in London," (wrote Francis Garden to Trench, November 26th, 1833,)

"I saw a letter from poor Alfred Tennyson. Both himself and his family seemed plunged in the deepest affliction."

The poet had been daily expecting to hear of his friend's return home,

> thinking ' here to-day '
> Or ' here to-morrow will he come.'

He likens himself to a mother praying for her sailor son the very moment

> His heavy-shotted hammock-shroud
> Drops in his vast and wandering grave,

or to a father pledging his gallant son in the wine cup while on the battlefield a shot still'd the life that beat from him.

> My blood an even tenor kept,
> Till on mine ear this message falls,
> That in Vienna's fatal walls
> God's finger touch'd him, and he slept.

Many have been the endeavours to discover the name of the "fair ship" which brought home Hallam's remains, and thus trace her after history, but all in vain. It seems, however, that she landed her precious freight at Dover, though the poet till a few years ago always believed she had put in to Bristol. From Dover the coffin was conveyed across country by coach to Clevedon Church, where in the manor aisle it was finally committed to its last resting place on the 3rd January, 1834.

This church was chosen by Mr. Hallam partly on account of its being the burial place of his son's maternal grandfather, Sir A. Elton, Bart. of Clevedon Court, and because of its sequestered situation.

It stands half a mile to the south of Clevedon, overlooking a broad expanse of water, where the

Snowdon Church.

Severn flows down into the Bristol Channel, and is so hidden that

> a stranger here
> Might wondering ask—Where stands the house of God?
> She sought it o'er the fields, and found at last
> An old and lonely church, beside the sea,
> In a green hollow 'twixt two headlands green.

To the highly-strung nervous temperament of Tennyson the burial of his friend was too trying an ordeal to face, so he was not present at the funeral. Few are now living who were there, but Augustus James, the old sexton of Clevedon Church, who when a boy witnessed the interment, still survives.

It was his father who dug the vault, into which was lowered not only the coffin but a square iron box containing

> 'The darken'd heart that beat no more.'

The day was fine, the hour of burial one o'clock, no flowers, no music, only the tolling of the large bell in the tower.

> Yet in these ears, till hearing dies,
> One set slow bell will seem to toll
> The passing of the sweetest soul
> That ever look'd with human eyes.

> I hear it now, and o'er and o'er,
> Eternal greetings to the dead ;
> And ' Ave, Ave, Ave,' said,
> ' Adieu, adieu ' for evermore.

It was several years after the burial before the poet saw Clevedon, but his visit made a lasting impression on his mind, so that even when time and distance intervened, the moonlight falling on his bed would cause his thoughts to revert to the dim old lonely church, where, when the moon is high in the heavens, it strikes through the large south window of the manor aisle, illuminating the tablet erected by the Historian to his son's memory:

> When on my bed the moonlight falls,
> I know that in thy place of rest
> By that broad water of the west,
> There comes a glory on the walls :
>
> Thy marble bright in dark appears,
> As slowly steals a silver flame
> Along the letters of thy name,
> And o'er the number of thy years.

The tablet is placed in the centre of the western wall of the aisle almost opposite the organ, underneath which is the vault where the body of Hallam lies; and the touching record of his short life, which the poet here represents as struggling into light under the moon's flickering rays, is penned as follows.

There are now four tablets in this part of the church, as three years after Arthur's death his sister Eleanor passed away, then followed his mother and his younger brother Henry, and in 1859 the Historian himself.

    HERE, WITH HIS WIFE AND CHILDREN, RESTS
       HENRY HALLAM, THE HISTORIAN

is the epitaph which the Laureate wrote on the last tablet.

IN MEMORIAM.

It was in May, 1850, that "In Memoriam" was given to the world, a few copies having been circulated among

the poet's personal friends in the previous year. The book did not bear the Author's name on the title page, but critics were agreed that no one but Tennyson could have written it. Strange to say, it did not meet with the universal approbation that is now conceded to it, what Dr. George Macdonald once styled "a brutal review" appearing in "The Times" under the title of "The Poetry of Sorrow."

During the seventeen years the poet was engaged writing his great masterpiece next to nothing is known of his haunts. He was living almost in another world, communing with its spirits, solving doubts, following problems to the verge of the Infinite.

Writing of this time, Howitt says—"It is very possible you may come across him in a country inn, with a foot on each hob of the fireplace, a volume of Greek in one hand, his meerschaum in the other, so far advanced towards the seventh heaven that he would not thank you to call him back into this nether world." This is a little indefinite, yet pretty near the truth, as there are few places during this period where his footsteps are distinctly visible.

It was in the early months of 1837 that the Tennysons left Somersby, and, in a letter to Monckton Milnes, dated January 10th, 1837, the poet makes touching reference to their expected departure.

"It is very problematical whether I shall be able to come and see you as I proposed, . . . and if I come I should only be able to stop a few days, for as I and all my people are going to leave this place very shortly never to return, I have much upon my hands."

Beech Hill House was the name of their new home, an old mansion—now pulled down and rebuilt—close to High Beech, a village on the verge of Epping Forest, in Essex.

As the name indicates, the house is situated on a hill, from which there is a fine view of Waltham Abbey and its surrounding hamlets lying in the hollow about two and a half miles distant. Waltham Abbey, or Waltham Holy Cross, is a place of great interest—its old Norman church (where the poet frequently worshipped) being famous for the

many associations which cling to it in connection with Harold, the last of the Saxon kings, and also for the splendid bells in the tower on which celebrated peals have been rung from time immemorial.

On Christmas Eve, in the vigil of midnight hours, the poet hears these bells pealing, and "sad memory brings the light of other days around him" as he thinks of the familiar bells of Somersby. Now all is changed—the old home broken up, the haunts of his youth forsaken, and he dwells "within the stranger's land."

> The time draws near the birth of Christ;
>   The moon is hid, the night is still;
>   A single church below the hill
> Is pealing, folded in the mist.
>
> A single peal of bells below,
>   That wakens at this hour of rest
>   A single murmur in the breast,
> That these are not the bells I know.

But a week elapses, and again he listens to the same bells ringing out the old year and ringing in the new. If they brought sadness to him before, they bring joy to him now, his spirits rising into a higher air and finding expression in jubilant song:

> Ring out the old, ring in the new,
>   Ring, happy bells, across the snow:
>   The year is going, let him go;
> Ring out the false, ring in the true.

No doubt one of the chief attractions High Beech had for the Tennysons was its vicinity to the Metropolis, it being so near that hither, it is said, Henry VIII. came, in order that he might be at a distance and still hear the guns from the tower announcing Anne Boleyn's death. To London, therefore, the poet resorted now more frequently than hitherto, and singularly interesting is the glimpse "In Memoriam" gives us of a visit he paid about this time to Hallam's old home at No. 67 Wimpole Street.

It was not the first time he had resorted there since his friend's death. Once before, on a dull wintry morning, overwhelmed with grief at the news which had just arrived, he had sought the "dark house" "in the long unlovely street"; now, more resigned to his loss, he revisits it on an early morning in spring, when there is a strange quiet charm about the city so foreign to it at other hours;

> Doors, where my heart was used to beat
> So quickly, not as one that weeps
> I come once more; the city sleeps;
> I smell the meadow in the street;
>
> I hear a chirp of birds; I see
> Betwixt the black fronts long-withdrawn
> A light-blue lane of early dawn,
> And think of early days and thee.

His fame was now growing apace, and no one was more eagerly welcomed in the select literary circles of London; but he shunned society, and, beyond a very small coterie, was never to be met, preferring "to sit up all night talking with a friend, or else to sit and think alone."

Occasionally he would spend an evening with his college set—a record of such a reunion being related by Fitzgerald in one of his letters to Bernard Barton. Writing from London in the spring of 1838, he says—

"We have had Alfred Tennyson here; very droll, and very wayward; and much sitting up of nights till two and three in the morning with pipes in our mouths: at which good hour we would get Alfred to give us some of his magic music, which he does between growling and smoking."

Mrs. Tennyson did not remain long at High Beech. The poet did not care for the district, complaining that there were no sounds of nature and a want of birds and men. So they left it about 1840 for Tunbridge Wells—the following year settling at Boxley, near Maidstone.

One of the beautiful mansions in this parish, commanding a magnificent stretch of Kentish scenery, is Park House, which has long been the seat of the Lushingtons, a family whom Milnes described as having "an hereditary right to, a sort of habit of, academic distinction."

The head of the family, Edmund Law Lushington, after being captain of Charterhouse School, went down to Cambridge during the halo of Tennyson's youthful celebrity. Here he was the first Grecian of his time, being senior medallist of his year, heading the list in the Classical Tripos and graduating Senior Optime

in mathematics. After being for a short time a fellow of Trinity College, he was appointed in 1838

to succeed Sir Daniel K. Sandford as Professor of Greek in the University of Glasgow, where, during a long and distinguished career, he was revered by all who had the privilege of his acquaintance, not only for his exact and erudite scholarship, but because

> he bore without abuse
> The grand old name of gentleman.

On 10th October, 1842, at Boxley, he was married to the poet's youngest sister, Miss Cecilia Tennyson—a record of this happy event being preserved for all time by the Epithalamium of "In Memoriam." In it the poet pays a well-deserved tribute to his brother-in-law's great abilities, the Professor being considered the most scholarly man in England after Bishop Thirlwall.

> And thou art worthy; full of power;
> As gentle; liberal-minded, great,
> Consistent; wearing all that weight
> Of learning lightly like a flower.

Professor Lushington, to whom the 85th ode of "In Memoriam" is addressed, watched the growth of the poem for several years; and it was to the Professor's younger brother, Henry, one of the few the poet consulted in literary matters, that Tennyson dedicated "The Princess," some of the description in the Prologue having been taken from Park House and from a meeting of the Maidstone Mechanics' Institute, held in the park, at which the poet was present.

> And me that morning Walter show'd the house,
> Greek, set with busts: from vases in the hall
> Flowers of all heavens, and lovelier than their names,
> Grew side by side; and on the pavement lay
> Carved stones of the Abbey-ruin in the park,
> Huge Ammonites, and the first bones of Time;
> And on the tables every clime and age
> Jumbled together; celts and calumets,
> Claymore and snowshoe, toys in lava, fans
> Of sandal, amber, ancient rosaries,
> Laborious orient ivory sphere in sphere,
> The cursed Malayan crease, and battle-clubs
> From the isles of palm: and higher on the walls,
> Betwixt the monstrous horns of elk and deer,
> His own forefathers' arms and armour hung.

It was during this period of his life that Tennyson formed the acquaintance of his great compeer in literature, Thomas Carlyle, and up the narrow street of Cheyne Row might he be seen wending his way during some of his brief visits to town.

IN MEMORIAM.

"One evening," says Mr. Froude, "when Carlyle came home from his walk, he found Tennyson sitting with Mrs. Carlyle in the garden, smoking comfortably."

He admired and almost loved Tennyson. He says:—"A fine, large-featured, dim-eyed, bronze-coloured, shaggy-headed man is Alfred; dusty, smoky, free and easy, who swims outwardly and inwardly with great composure in an articulate element of tranquil chaos and tobacco smoke. Great now and then when he does emerge — a most restful, brotherly, solid-hearted man."

Such a visitor cheered the heart of Carlyle, who delighted in his companionship; but the poet's visits were fewer than he could have wished, as Tennyson came less and less frequently to town, the family having removed further from London—Boxley being exchanged for Cheltenham in 1844.

This year was memorable for the rise of a new star on the literary horizon—Ruskin having just published his first volume of "Modern Painters." The book was published anonymously; and, strangely neglected by the leading reviewers, its reception, as one has remarked, was simply contemptuous. Tennyson, however, who had noticed it lying on Rogers' table in London was not slow to discern that the book was no common one, and that the author, whoever he might be, was a man of powerful and original intellect, so, writing in 1844 from 10 St. James's Square, Cheltenham, he asked Moxon to send him a copy.

> Another book I long very much to see is that on the superiority of the Modern Painters to the old ones & the greatness of Turner as an artist. by an Oxford undergraduate I think

The attraction of these great minds was mutual, for if Carlyle declared that Tennyson alone proved singing to be possible in our curt English speech, Ruskin shared in his master's admiration of the Laureate's genius.

Repeatedly in "Modern Painters" he quotes passages from the poet's works, now a line of "In Memoriam," now a stanza from "Maud," to illustrate some of the great truths he is desirous of impressing on the minds of his readers, and not long after he

had settled at Brantwood, his beautiful home on Coniston Lake, he wrote with characteristic generosity these celebrated and oft-quoted words:—

"No description that I have ever given of anything is worth four lines of Tennyson; and in serious thought, my half-pages are generally only worth about as much as a single sentence of his."

Tennyson, Carlyle, and Ruskin—the Poet, the Historian, and the Prose-Bard—will always be linked together as the three great masters in literature of the nineteenth century.

They are a noble trio, the flower of their age, whose lives are not less heroic than their works.

There is one trait in their characters common to all of them which is worthy of remark, namely, their filial devotion.

Each was blessed with pious parents, each had the advantage of a Puritanic upbringing, hence that spirit of reverence so noticeable in all their writings.

> Thrice blest whose lives are faithful prayers,
> Whose loves in higher love endure;
> What souls possess themselves so pure,
> Or is their blessedness like theirs?

The poet's father was cut off just as he was discerning the universality of his son's mind, but his mother lived to see her son "chapleted with laurel" by his admiring countrymen.

With her at Cheltenham Tennyson dwelt mostly from 1844 till 1850, for it was some time after the publication of "In Memoriam" that she took up her residence at Well Walk, Hampstead, where she passed away in her 85th year.

She does not rest beside her husband in the quiet churchyard at Somersby, near the old rectory, where she trained her boys, but hard by the entrance of Highgate Cemetery a small cross—

> The symbol of the holiest death of all,

marks her grave, under it being carved simply the words—

Elizabeth
Tennyson,
FEB. 21st, 1865.

Marriage.

"These two—they dwelt with eye on eye,
 Their hearts of old have beat in tune,
 Their meetings made December June,
 Their every parting was to die."

MARRIAGE.

Love may be said to be the key-note of Tennyson. It is his favourite harp-string; he never wearies sounding it, from his "Airy, fairy Lilian" down to his latest ode,—with him "no lapse of moons can canker Love."

The poet, he tells us, is dowered with "the love of love," which, whether or not an unfailing characteristic, seems in any case true of Tennyson, as the spirit of his poems abundantly testifies.

Love, however, which finds its realization in marriage, could in his early years only be looked forward to by him; for, unlike his squire in "The Miller's Daughter," he had few broad acres to call his own, having accepted the spirit of poetry as his fortune and chosen for himself a difficult path up the hill of Parnassus, whose bare slopes yield but scanty subsistence. Thus the greater part of Tennyson's early

MARRIAGE.

manhood was passed unmarried, living with his friends and his golden dreams.

During all these years he was never idle, but ever moving upwards, cultivating by great study his marvellous intellect.

With the publication of "In Memoriam" in May 1850 the seed was sown broadcast through the land, and the same year brought the golden harvest. This year may be said to have been the crowning one of the poet's life. The world lay at his feet, the Laureateship within his grasp—the cultivated youth of the universities hanging on his every utterance with

absolute idolatry. Rest and honour had now come to him, and so the dreams of his youth might be said to be realized.

In the centre of the picturesque town of Horncastle stands a square red-brick mansion, which in the early part of the century was the home of Mr. Henry Sellwood. He was a country gentleman, belonging to one of the oldest county families in Berkshire and Somersetshire, and was engaged at Horncastle in the profession of a solicitor. His wife, who was a sister of the 'heroic sailor' Sir John Franklin, after giving birth to three daughters, fell a prey in early life to consumption. Hard by in the large parish church one almost unconsciously walks over her grave, which bears this inscription—

IN MEMORY OF
SARAH,
WIFE OF HENRY SELLWOOD,
WHO DEPARTED THIS LIFE
ON THE 30TH DAY OF SEPTEMBER, 1816,
AGED 28 YEARS.

As Horncastle was the nearest market town to Somersby, and the young Sellwoods and Tennysons were of an age, a friendship naturally existed between the two families which in after years ripened into a double relationship—the poet's elder brother, Charles, marrying the youngest and the poet himself the eldest daughter, Emily Sarah Sellwood.

Charles' nuptials were solemnized at Horncastle, but Tennyson was married in Shiplake Church,

Oxfordshire—a fitting place for a poet to be wedded in, occupying, as it does, one of the most charming situations on a bend of the "silver-streaming" Thames.

The marriage took place on 13th June 1850, the clergyman who officiated being the late Rev. Robert Drummond Burrell Rawnsley, a Lincolnshire man, and intimate friend of the Laureate, who was a frequent guest at the vicarage—and wrote that beautiful ode of "In Memoriam" commencing "Sad Hesper o'er the buried sun" while staying under the vicar's hospitable roof at Shiplake.

From a letter of Carlyle to his wife, dated September 1850, we get a glimpse of the newly-wedded couple on a visit at Tent Lodge, Coniston.

"Alfred looks really improved, I should say; cheerful in what he talks, and looking forward to a future less detached than the past has been. A good soul, find him where and how situated you may. Mrs. Tennyson lights up bright glittering blue eyes when you speak to her; has wit, has sense; and were it not that she seems so very delicate in health, I should augur really well of Tennyson's adventure."

Carlyle was right in his prognostications; for,

unlike some of the great literary figures of the nineteenth century, the Laureate has been peculiarly happy in his married life.

In the dedication of "Enoch Arden" he refers to Lady Tennyson as

> Dear, near and true—no truer Time himself
> Can prove you, tho' he make you evermore
> Dearer and nearer,

and to her, says Mr. Palgrave, "he has never looked in vain for aid and comfort, the Wife whose perfect love has blessed him through these many years with large and faithful sympathy."

Chapel House, Twickenham, was the home Tennyson brought his bride to, and where he spent the first three years of his married life.

It is a corner house in Montpelier Row, a terrace running betwixt the Thames and the Richmond Road, about the same distance east as Pope's Villa is west of Twickenham. Time has allowed creepers to cover the walls, but the original character of the house remains unchanged—the poet's study, known as the Green Room, where he wrote his superb "Ode on the Death of the Duke of Wellington," being left in much the same condition as when he occupied it.

It was at Chapel House in 1852 that the poet's eldest son was born, the Hon. Hallam Tennyson, who for

many years has been his father's constant companion, accompanying him in his travels and shielding him in every possible way from the cares and worries which necessarily fall to the lot of the "Dean of the literary guild." "He had his son Hallam with him," wrote Fitzgerald (after a visit the Laureate paid him at Woodbridge), "whom I liked much: unaffected and unpretentious: so attentive to his father, with a humorous sense of his character as well as a loving and respectful. It was good to see them together."

The poet's younger son, Mr. Lionel Tennyson, was born at Farringford in 1854. He bore a strong resemblance to the Laureate, inheriting much of his father's literary ability and love of humour.

Having a strong natural leaning to Oriental subjects, he entered the Political and Secret Department of the India Office, where he soon distinguished himself by drawing up an admirable report on the "Moral and Material Progress and Condition of India for 1881-2."

On the invitation of Lord Dufferin, then Viceroy of India, he made a prolonged tour through our great Eastern Empire, which, alas! proved too much for his constitution, as there

> In haunts of jungle-poison'd air
> The flame of life went wavering down.

"We left Calcutta very early this morning," writes Lady Dufferin, March 30th, 1886. "Poor Mr. Tennyson's bed was pulled to the window that he might see us off. He is still very ill, but as the hot weather is coming on he must go home, and he is to start on Sunday. He has had a long, sad illness, borne most patiently."

Accompanied by his wife (the brilliant and cultured

daughter of Mr. Locker-Lampson), he embarked for home in the *Chusan*, on board of which he died near Aden, and, like Wilkie, was buried at sea.

Three little boys survive him, the eldest of whom is the

> Golden-hair'd Ally whose name is one with mine,
> Crazy with laughter and babble and earth's new wine,
> . . . . .
> Glorious poet who never hast written a line.

Farringford.

"It lies
Deep-meadow'd, happy, fair with orchard-lawns
And bowery hollows crown'd with summer sea."

X

FARRINGFORD.

FARRINGFORD, in the Isle of Wight, is inseparably bound up with the name of Tennyson. It is situated in the parish of Freshwater, which again is in the extreme south-west of the primrose isle, where the land begins to narrow down between the waters of the Solent and the Channel.

Forty years ago Freshwater was a very different place from what it is now. It was then a quiet, rural parish, unspotted with villas, where news from the great world only came at stated intervals; for while other portions of the island could be reached easily enough, access to this part depended very much on the irregular sailings of a little vessel crossing the Solent at Yarmouth, "which, when it crossed," says one who lived there at that time, "we got letters, and when it did not cross we went without." The population being sparse, the only houses were the mansions of those families who owned the soil, and a handful of cottages for their dependants.

One of these mansions was Farringford, described as an old house with a rambling garden at the back of the downs. Before the poet's occupancy it was let to an eminent judge, who made it his summer residence. On his leaving it, the place was offered for sale, and the Laureate, attracted by the picturesqueness of the surrounding country, purchased it, and here in the fall of 1853 he settled down with his wife and child.

About seventeen years prior to this time Monckton Milnes had asked the poet to become one of the contributors to the *Tribute*, an annual in which he was interesting himself; and Tennyson, always willing to oblige his friends, made the book a success by writing for it, what Trench, a fellow contributor, called the "magnificent" stanzas, beginning —

> Oh! that 'twere possible,
>   After long grief and pain,
> To find the arms of my true-love
>   Round me once again!

This fragment had never been republished, but had

lain hidden away in this miscellany, and was almost forgotten. Shortly after taking up his residence at Farringford, the poet read the lines to his neighbour, Sir John Simeon, who remarked that it seemed to him as if something were wanting to explain the story of the poem; and, acting on his suggestion, Tennyson determined to put the jewel in a proper setting.

Time and place were propitious for the composition of such a work. The poet was happy in his new surroundings, the beautiful locality where he now dwelt, with its delightful blending of sea and country, acting as a stimulus to his mind, while the quiet uninterrupted evenings afforded him an opportunity for study better perhaps than he had enjoyed for some time.

Under these favourable circumstances "Maud" was written, a poem which might be called the poet's poem, it being in his own opinion one of the finest of his creations.

It was, however, only the prelude of greater works to follow; for Tennyson, unlike those who are afraid to embark on some new enterprise lest they may wreck their past reputation, was ever seeking a newer world wherein to find fresh scope for the versatility of his genius.

The love he had as a boy for the ancient records of English chivalry had already found expression in such poems as the " Lady of Shalott," " Sir Launcelot and Queen Guinevere," and the " Morte d'Arthur." These, however, were, like the stanzas contributed to the *Tribute*, merely detached fragments, and to weave them into one grand epic was the goal the poet now set before him. The labour involved was such as might have staggered the determination of a much younger man, and Mr. Gladstone very truly has said that Tennyson " will bequeath to us at least one lesson in the loyalty, constancy, and intensity of his devotion to his calling," for the " Idylls of the King," commenced after the meridian of his life was past, were not completed till he had reached beyond the threescore and ten years which sum up the ordinary span of human life.

During the time occupied in writing these " Idylls," the seclusion the poet so dearly valued at Freshwater gradually became a thing of the past, and Tennyson in causing the aged Merlin to say—

Sweet were the days when I was all unknown,

may have been betraying his own feelings, as now that his fame encircled the globe, Farringford became one of the most overrun spots in Europe, people lurking about the shrubberies, staring in at his windows, and watching him as he walked out of his gates.

Besides these unbidden visitors, many of the most notable literary and scientific men of the century, such as Maurice, Kingsley, Dean Stanley, Darwin, Herschel, and many others—giants in their different walks—have been the poet's guests at one time or other at Farringford.

Opening the door to a caller, the servant sees a tall, handsome gentleman, who on learning that the poet was not at home, and being asked for his name, replies, " Merely say Prince Albert called."

Garibaldi, fresh from his victories on the blood-red battlefields of Italy, plants a tree of Liberty in the avenue leading up to the house, while hither also comes Longfellow, free from all taint of jealousy, and amid the pine groves of Farringford holds such converse with 'the many-sided mind' of its owner, that on his return to his native land, he writes an ode to the " sweet historian of the heart "—

> in sign
> Of homage to the mastery, which is thine,
> In English song.

FARRINGFORD.

The opening words of "Enoch Arden"—

> Long lines of cliff breaking have left a chasm ;
> And in the chasm are foam and yellow sands ;

while describing a purely imaginary locality is not

unlike a picture of the scenery at Freshwater Bay. The downs on which the poet loves to ramble, and every foot of which is classic ground, suddenly dip down to a little cove, and then as suddenly rise again.

Proceeding inland from this bay, the road skirts a

number of new houses, the erection of which must have cost the poet many a pang, as he apostrophizes them in the trenchant lines—

Yonder lies our young sea-village—Art and Grace are less and
　　less:
Science grows and Beauty dwindles—roofs of slated hideous-
　　ness!

Opposite these new villas stands the ivy-clad house so long occupied by Mrs. Julia Cameron, the celebrated lady art-photographer, whose effective portraits of Tennyson and of other great men whom she posed in her studio are well known.

Passing onward, the road is joined by Farringford Lane, a shady path down which the poet often comes when walking from his house to the sea.

At this junction the policies of Farringford commence. No stiff stone wall encloses them, but a high natural bank, surmounted by a hedge, screens them from the main road. Here and there a gap in this 'wall of green' lays bare to view the park, charmingly varied with clusters of large trees and deep pasture; but a glimpse of the 'woodland paradise' itself is scarcely obtainable, on account of the impenetrable foliage which surrounds it.

The entrance to the park is so simple that strangers might almost pass without noticing it. This is partly due to the situation of the gardener's lodge, as it does not stand within the park, but on the other side of the road, opposite the entrance gateway—its

windows looking over to the avenue which terminates a hundred yards or so further on, at the glass-panelled doors of the Laureate's home.

No better words could be used to describe Farringford, than Miss Thackeray's when she calls it, "a charmed palace, with green walls without, and speaking walls within," for outside there is scarcely a foot of masonry which is not covered with the most luxuriant creepers, while indoors the rooms are lined with books from floor to ceiling.

As at Somersby, the poet's study is in the topmost

storey of the house, while on a level with the lawn, where the cedar spreads 'his dark-green layers of shade' is the drawing room. This room, with its oriel window looking out over the park to the sea,

is the one where the poet would sometimes melt the eyes of his guests, as in the fading light he read in his deep-toned voice some passage of touching pathos from his own works. Not many pictures adorn the walls, but over the mantel hangs a fine engraving of Sebastiano del Piombo's masterpiece—Christ raising Lazarus, recalling the lines—

> Behold a man raised up by Christ !
> The rest remaineth unreveal'd ;
> He told it not ; or something seal'd
> The lips of that Evangelist.

Nowhere is Tennyson more at home than in a garden. Open his poems where we please, we are sure to find some allusion to flowers, plants, and trees, couched in language which, for choiceness of epithet, is not surpassed by Shakespeare.

As might therefore be expected, the grounds round Farringford, having been laid out by Lady Tennyson and the poet, are, for beauty and picturesqueness, all that could be desired.

On the south side of the house the eye wanders down a lovely glade, to which Miss Thackeray makes reference when she says, "There is a photograph I have always liked, in which it seems to me the history of this home is written. It was taken in the green glade at Farringford. Hallam and Lionel Tennyson stand on either side of their parents, the sun is shining, and no doubt the thrushes and robins are singing and fluttering in the wind-blown branches of the trees, as the father and mother and the children come advancing towards us."

Close to this glade grow some of the poet's rarest trees, one of the most interesting being

> the waving pine which here
> The warrior of Caprera set.

The Laureate has all a poet's love for trees, and the pleasure he takes in watching the growth of his own is evident from some of the verses in one of his latest poems, entitled "To Ulysses." "He took delight," says Oliver Wendell Holmes, "in pointing out to me the finest and rarest of his trees, and there were many beauties among them. In this garden of England, where everything grows with such a lavish extravagance of green, I felt as if weary eyes and over-tasked brains might reach their happiest haven of rest."

Passing down through trim-kept walks, "the dry-tongued laurel" forming a rampart on either side, a gate opens on a large walled garden. A proof of the mildness of the climate is not wanting, as here figs may be seen growing outside. The air smells sweet with the fragrance of alleys of rosebushes, while the rooks calling "Maud, Maud, Maud, Maud," make music in the high branches of the surrounding trees.

In his well-known invitation to Maurice he speaks thus pleasantly of his house and its surroundings—

>Where, far from noise and smoke of town,
>I watch the twilight falling brown
>All round a careless-order'd garden
>Close to the ridge of a noble down.

FARRINGFORD.

This down has fittingly been called Tennyson's Down, partly because it forms part of the Farringford

estate, partly on account of its being the poet's out-of-doors study, where he has spent many days and nights in contemplative thought.

As the hills and dales, lakes and streams round Rydal Mount inspired Wordsworth, so this "hushed companionable down" has often invigorated the mind of Tennyson.

A stroll along its lofty ridge is still the poet's favourite walk, and, when residing at Farringford, he may almost daily be seen climbing the steep combe of the chalk cliff, and passing, like his own Lancelot,

Far o'er the long backs of the bushless downs.

On the highest part of the down stands Farringford Beacon, the cliffs here rising to the height of 483 feet above the sea-level. The Beacon only serves as a landmark by day, for no light is displayed upon its wooden turret at night, but it serves another useful purpose,

as it is the visitor's book of this locality, the supports and even the turf on which it stands being cut and carved with the names and initials of the Laureate's numerous admirers. The ascent to it from Freshwater Bay is by no means so easy as at first appears, especially if a south-westerly gale happens to be blowing in from the Atlantic; but once the goal is reached, the toil is repaid by a magnificent view, the whole peninsula lying stretched out beneath.

Looking inland we see in the foreground the "groves of pine" round the poet's home; beyond, smiling hamlets dot the landscape at various points, while far in the distance the river Yar can be traced, now spreading itself out like a lake beneath the

old Parish Church of Freshwater, now creeping onward through reedy meadows till it joins the waters of the Solent.

Turning our eyes seaward, as we look out o'er the "far-rolling, west-ward-smiling seas," and watch the white-maned waves chasing each other before the wind, some of Tennyson's marvellous descriptions of the sea rise in our memory.

The representative poet of a great maritime nation like England should be a lover of the sea, and certainly in this respect, the Laureate is not found lacking. From childhood the world of waters has been to him a special object of love and joy, and the intense passion for the sea, which caused him when a boy to run bareheaded all the way from Somersby to the Lincolnshire coast, has increased rather than diminished with years.

At Farringford his study windows are so situated that from them he can watch the long waves rolling into Freshwater Bay, and one of the attractions of Aldworth is, that though so far inland, it yet commands "one gray glimpse of sea."

On the approach of summer few things delight the poet more than to cruise along the southern coast of England in a "Sunbeam" or an "Assegai," and his periodical crossing of the Solent in the "Mayflower" is always enjoyed by him, and is said to have called forth one of his latest and finest lyrics, "Crossing the Bar."

It is not surprising then when we turn to his poems to find them replete with the most exquisite allusions to the sea—in its ever-changing aspects, and to the stirring events connected with it.

Perhaps his most popular poem is that touching story of sailor life, "Enoch Arden"; perhaps his grandest simile that in "The Last Tournament," where he compares the fall of the Red Knight to a great wave spending its way along some sandy seaboard.

The poet's minute and accurate observations of the landward beauties of nature has often been remarked on by his friends, and to some extent this has also been the case with his allusions to the sea, as instance of which might be noted Mr. Swinburne's criticism of the line in "The Marriage of Geraint,"

> And white sails flying on the yellow sea.

"I could not but feel conscious," he says, "at once of its charm and of the equally certain fact that I, though cradled and reared beside the sea, had never seen anything like that. But on the first bright day I ever spent on the eastern coast of England I saw the truth of this touch at once, and recognized once more with admiring delight the subtle and sure fidelity of that happy and studious hand. There, on the dull yellow foamless floor of dense discoloured sea, so thick with clotted sand that the water looked massive and solid as the shore, the white sails flashed whiter against it and along it as they fled;

and I knew once more the truth of what I never had doubted—that the eye and the hand of Tennyson may always be trusted, at once and alike, to see and to express the truth."

Beyond the Beacon, westwards, there is a slight declivity in the down, followed by a long stretch of level turf for more than a mile, after which the "tender-tinted cliffs" gradually dip and dip downward, till they reach a point in the rocks and lighthouse well known to mariners as the Needles.

Returning by more frequented paths, we at once know when we are within the marches of the poet's estate from the many neat little cottages peeping out amid bowers of honeysuckle, with a monogram of the letters A. E. T. (Alfred and Emily Tennyson) cut in a red stone over the doorway, " labourers' homes " "each a nest in bloom," such as Edith Aylmer delighted to visit when on her rounds of mercy.

The Home Farm, with its thatched roof and "martin-haunted eaves," may be taken as a type of these picturesque abodes, whose simple rusticity strikes the traveller, when he contrasts it with the shoddiness of more pretentious villas which mar the landscape in other parts of the parish, making him wish for those olden times,

When men knew how to build.

Aldworth.

"You came, and look'd and loved the view
  Long-known and loved by me,
Green Sussex fading into blue
  With one gray glimpse of sea."

ALDWORTH.

THE erection of so many new houses destroying his privacy at Freshwater, and Lady Tennyson's health requiring stronger air, induced the poet, about a quarter of a century ago, to seek an additional residence, where he could have more retirement and a less relaxing climate than was possible at Farringford during the summer months.

The undulating elegance of the borderlands of Surrey, with their green wooded slopes and dark stretches of moor and heath, had not escaped his keen perception of rural beauty; and in the autumn of 1866, accompanied by his wife, he called on Mrs. Anne Gilchrist, at Brookbank, near Shotter Mill, the very heart of this lovely district, with a view to inspecting a neighbouring property called the 'Jumps,' which was then for sale.

The place did not please the poet, but the country round Brookbank being quite to his mind, he rented Grayshott on the top of Hindhead Farm, to see if the climate suited Lady Tennyson's health, and to be on the watch for any land that should be in the market.

After looking at several places, such as Hurt Hill and Mead Fields, the Laureate purchased the estate of Green Hill, situated really in Sussex, though only half a mile or so across the border line which separates that county from Surrey.

"Yes," writes Mrs. Gilchrist, July, 1867, "we succeeded at last in finding land to suit. It is a wooded hollow in Blackdown, at once very sheltered, for the hill curves round on either side and rises sheer behind it to the north, so that it is like a little bay; yet elevated, and commanding the view you know well—Surrey, Sussex, parts of Hampshire, and, I suppose, part of Kent, South Downs. I do think, if ever there was a place made for a poet to live in, this Green Hill, as it is called, is the spot."

On this site Aldworth (called after one of the old Sellwood demesnes) was built, and since 1869 it has been the custom of the poet to quit Farringford about June, and, crossing the Solent in the 'Mayflower,' reside here till late autumn, when he returns to his island home.

The nearest post town is Haslemere, lying in a

hollow of the Surrey hills, a village which has in recent years become quite a centre of cultured society.

Poetry is represented by the Laureate, Science by Tyndall, Fiction by Mrs. Humphry Ward ; while many artists such as Tadema, Boughton, and Du Maurier are often to be found sojourning in the vicinity. It was to Haslemere that John Burroughs came that he might hear the nightingale sing, and in his amusing essay he describes the country round about as " wild and irregular, full of lovely fields and over-grown hedgerows and very nightingaly."

Aldworth is distant about two miles from Haslemere, but in this short space the road passes through very varied scenery. After traversing a fine English highway, and clambering over a rough common covered with whin bushes, a long winding lane is

reached, which enjoys the title of Tennyson's Lane, as the poet is often to be met walking here. The trees, which form an arch over it, suddenly disappear, and we come to a lone moor where not a sound is heard, and the line rings in our ears—

> Calm and deep peace on this high wold.

The road then divides into two paths, one dipping down into a deep gorge, the other leading over the brow of the hill. The latter has a sign-post with "private road" marked on it, and following it for two or three hundred yards we reach Aldworth.

Architecture has always been a favourite study with the Tennysons as a family. Dr. Tennyson imitated the Gothic long before even professional architects of the present day adopted this style of building, while his brother was a perfect adept at the art, as Bayons Manor testifies. This family talent is strongly developed in the poet, for in "The Princess," "Recollections of the Arabian Nights," "The Palace of Art," etc., one cannot but be struck with his knowledge of architecture, and with his fanciful descriptions of what might be called 'castles in the air,' picturing by a single stroke of his pen the style of a building; as when he speaks of the Abbey-ruin in Sir Walter Vivian's park being

> High-arch'd and ivy-claspt,
> Of finest Gothic lighter than a fire.

In Aldworth these imaginary designs have been realized in stone and lime. The plans were drawn by Mr. Knowles, the editor of the *Nineteenth Century*, the architecture being a free treatment of domestic Gothic of the Tudor period, but the poet superintended every detail, believing in what Mr. Ruskin says, that "there is a sanctity in a good man's house," and that it is "an evil sign of a people when their houses are built to last for one generation only."

Around the edifice runs a band of leaves carven in stone, interlacing the inscription (in Latin), 'Glory to God in the highest, and on earth peace, good will toward men'; whilst a Welsh motto, "*Y Gwir yn erbyn y byd*" ('The Truth against the World') is set into the tiles of the hall. The poet's study is in the west corner of the second story, and has two large windows, one, at which he works, looking westward over the pine glen, the other embracing a magnificent prospect to the south.

During his summer residence at this mansion, Lord Tennyson leads a very retired life, though he is not now so much of a recluse as he once was. Like Milton, whom he resembles in many respects, he knows the value of early rising, and devotes the freshest hours of the day to work. At noon he generally starts for his daily two hours' walk, and if one is abroad on Blackdown at that time he may chance to

hear his "broad-blown" voice and see his stately figure as he descends the private road accompanied by his son and his dogs.

It is his habit when out walking seldom to look at any one, but gazing on the ground to pass on lost in reverie, hence a stranger has not much chance of seeing the steel-coloured light which gleams in the poet's eye. Erect by nature, the burden of eighty years has caused him to stoop slightly, which takes away from his great height. A broad-brimmed hat covers his lofty brow, such part of his face as is visible being deeply furrowed with lines of thought.

In dress there is little to distinguish him from others save this hat and the Byronic collar.

Seldom now-a-days is he to be seen in Haslemere, though one may occasionally catch a glimpse of him driving through the village with Lady Tennyson, as the distance is rather far for him to walk, and so he usually confines his strolls to his own estate.

Though his fame is world-wide, its roots strike deepest round his own home; and as at Freshwater, so at Haslemere, he is held in the greatest respect by high and low.

In the welfare of those around him he is deeply interested, and though, with his retiring nature, all crowds are more or less distasteful, he sacrifices his own feelings and makes a point of being present at such gatherings as the local flower show and sports held in the grounds of Lythehill, the seat of his neighbour, Mr. Stewart Hodgson.

At his summer home he carries out his own noble maxim expressed in the lines—

> Why should not these great Sirs
> Give up their parks some dozen times a year
> To let the people breathe?

for it is not an uncommon occurrence to see one of his carriages driving from the station filled with "city children" who, under the charge of the Hon.

Mrs. Hallam Tennyson, are on their way to Aldworth for a day's enjoyment in the country.

> "They that can wander at will where the works of the Lord are reveal'd
> Little guess what joy can be got from a cowslip out of the field."

Many of the poet's personal friends, such as the Duke of Argyll, the Marquis of Dufferin, Aubrey de Vere, the Bishop of Ripon, Mr. Jowett, Professor Palgrave, Sir Alfred Lyall, visit him when residing at Aldworth, the place being within easy access of London by rail, and usually once a year he pays a visit of a few days duration to the 'dark Queen-city,' when he dines with Mr. Gladstone and some old friends. But the brilliant society of the Metropolis, which was so fascinating to Browning, has little attraction for the Laureate, as he loves far more

> His own gray towers, plain life and letter'd peace,
> To read and rhyme in solitary fields,
> The lark above, the nightingale below,
> And answer them in song.

Here, then, in his twilight-haunted study, we take our leave of him reading some old book, with his old hound couched by his side, in the hope that the manuscript lying on his table will soon be given to the world

> A flower all gold,
> And bravely furnish'd all abroad to fling
> The winged shafts of truth,
> To throng with stately blooms the breathing spring
> Of Hope and Youth.

Index.

"Summ'd up and closed in little."

INDEX.

Abbotsford, 79.
Aden, 63, 160.
"Airy, fairy Lilian," 153.
Aldworth, 179, 186, 188, 189, 193.
Alford, 38.
Alford, Dean, 123.
Allen, 83.
'Apostles, The,' 125.
Ardrossan, 57.
Argyll, Duke of, 193.
Arnold, Matthew, 38.
Ashestiel, 79.
"Assegai, The," 179.
"Aylmer's Field," 66, 90.
Ayrshire, 57.

Barbadoes, 75.
Barton, Bernard, 141.
Bag-Enderby, 5, 26, 34, 35, 36.
Bag-Enderby Church, 36.
Bag-Enderby Church Font, 36.
Battell, Rev. Ralph, 27.
"Battle of Armageddon," 124.

Baumber, John, 88.
Bayons Manor, 64, 67, 71, 74, 75, 189.
Beck, 35.
Bede, Cuthbert, 49.
Beech Hill House, 137.
Bell Scholarship, 47.
Bentley, 7.
Berkshire, 155.
Blackdown, 186, 190.
Bletchingley, 74.
Bolas, 104, 108.
Bolas Church, 106.
Bolas Villa, 107.
Boleyn, Anne, 140.
"Bonnie Doon," 58.
Boston Church, 11.
Boughton, 187.
Boxley, 142, 143, 147.
Brabant, 86.
Brantwood, 148.
"Break, break, break," 51.
Bristol 132.

INDEX

Bristol Channel, 133.
Brookbank, 185, 186.
Brookfield, 123.
Browning, 193.
Buller, 125.
"Buoy-Bell, The," 53.
Burghley, 111.
Burleigh, 107.
Burleigh House, 73, 103, 111, 112, 113.
Burns, 53, 57, 58, 79.
Burroughs, John, 187.
Burton family, 5.
Burton, Rev. Langhorne Burton, 9, 29.
Byron, 43, 79.

Caistor, 48, 49, 64.
Caistorians, 49.
Calcutta, 159.
Cam, The, 120, 121.
Cambridge, 15, 47, 50, 67, 74, 81, 93, 118, 119, 121, 122, 124, 128, 142.
Cambridge Conversazione Society, 125.
Cameron, Mrs. Julia, 169.
Cannock Chase, 109.
Carlo Dolci, 113.
Carlyle, 83, 145, 146, 147, 149, 156.
Carlyle, Mrs., 102, 146.
Cecil, Henry, 104, 107, 108, 113.
Cecil, Lady Sophia, 113, 114.
Cecil, Sir William, 111.

Cecils, 110.
Champion, The, 96.
Chancellor's Medal, 123.
Chapel House, 157, 158.
Charterhouse, 142.
Cheltenham, 59, 147, 149.
Cheyne Row, 145.
China, 75.
Christ raising Lazarus, 173.
"Christian Year, The," 47.
"Chusan," The, 160.
Clark, Jonathan, 36, 37.
Clevedon, 132.
Clevedon Church, 132, 133, 134.
Clevedon Court, 132.
Coleridge, 48.
Conholt-Park, 114.
Coniston, 148, 156.
Corpus Buildings, 118.
Corpus Christi College, 118.
Crabbe, 37.
Crimean War, 75.
"Crossing the Bar," 179.
Cumberland, 3.

"Daphne and other Poems," 41.
"Days and Hours," 41.
Darwin, 167.
De Quincey, 43.
De Vere, Aubrey, 193.
Dean of the Literary Guild, 158.
"Death of the old Year, The," 49.
Descent of Tennyson, 71.

INDEX.

D'Eyncourt, Right Hon. Charles Tennyson, 71, 74.
D'Eyncourt, Admiral Edwin Clayton, 74, 75.
D'Eyncourt, Eustace Tennyson, 75.
D'Eyncourt, George Hildeyard, 75.
D'Eyncourt, Louis Charles, 72, 76.
D'Eyncourts, 66.
Dickens, 102.
Donne, 130.
Dover, 131, 132.
Dufferin, Lady, 159.
Dufferin, Lord, 63, 159, 193.
Du Maurier, 187.
Durham, 3.
Dymokes, 96, 97.

Edinburgh, 79.
Edith Aylmer, 182.
Edward III., 71.
Elton, Sir A., Bart., 132.
Emerson, 83.
England, 3, 18, 43, 54, 96, 103, 104, 108, 111, 112, 175, 179, 180.
"Enoch Arden," 157, 168, 179.
Epping Forest, 137.
Essex, 137.
Eton, 123.
Eton Miscellany, 123.
"Euphranor," 58.
Europe, 167.
"Eustace," 71, 73.

Eversley, 47.
Exeter, Countess of, 111, 113.
Exeter, Earl of, 104, 108.
Exeter, Marquis of, 103, 110, 113.
Exeter Family, 104.

Farringford, 54, 159, 163, 164, 165, 167, 170, 171, 173, 176, 179, 185, 186.
Farringford Beacon, 177, 181.
Farringford Home Farm, 182.
Farringford Lane, 169.
Fitzgerald, 58, 83, 103, 141, 158.
Flodden, 97.
Forêt de Soignies, 86.
Franklin, Sir John, 155.
Freshwater, 163, 166, 185, 192.
Freshwater Bay, 168, 177, 179.
Freshwater Parish Church, 178.
Froude, Mr., 146.
Fytche, Miss, 6.

Garden, Francis, 130.
Garibaldi, 167.
George III., 4.
George IV., 97.
German Ocean, 5.
Germany, 129, 130.
Gilchrist, Mrs. Anne, 185, 186.
Gladstone, Mr., 123, 127, 166, 193.
Glasgow University, 143.
"Godiva," 103.
Golden-hair'd Ally, 160.

Grasby, 49, 50, 53, 54, 58, 60, 67.
Grasby Church, 41.
Gray, 121.
Grayshott, 186.
Green Hill, 186.
Grimsby, Great, 64, 71, 74.
Gulf of Finland, 75.

Hagworthingham, 94.
Hallam, Arthur Henry, 8, 92, 117, 118, 122, 123, 125, 126, 127, 128, 130, 131, 134, 140.
Hallam, Eleanor, 135.
Hallam, Henry, 132, 135.
Hampshire, 186.
Hampstead, 150.
"Harold," 74.
Harold, 138.
Harrington Church, 95.
Harrington Hall, 95.
Haslemere, 60, 187, 188, 192.
Hawthorne, 4.
Hazlitt, 110.
Henry VIII., 3, 140.
Herschel, 167.
High Beech, 137, 140, 142.
Highgate Cemetery, 150.
High Street, 65.
Hilary, Sir Edward, 98.
Hindhead Farm, 186.
Hodgson, Stewart, 192.
Hoggins, Mr., 105.
Holmes, Oliver Wendell, 175.
Horncastle, 4, 11, 154, 155.

House of Commons, 74.
Howitt, 80, 137.
Hursley, 47.
Hurt Hill, 186.

"Idylls of the King," 166.
India, 159.
Ingilbys, 94.
"In Memoriam," 8, 15, 94, 136, 140, 144, 148, 150, 154, 156.
"Isles of Greece, The," 41.
Isle of Wight, 54, 163.
Italy, 54, 111, 167.

Jackson, Messrs., 44.
James, Augustus, 133.
James I., 112.
Jones, Mr., 106.
Jowett, Mr., 193.
'Jumps,' The, 185.

Keble, 47.
Kemble, 123, 124.
Kent South Downs, 186.
Kerr, Dr., 59.
King Alfred, 103.
Kinglake, 123.
Kingsley, 47, 82, 167.
King's College, 119.
Knowles, Mr., 189.

"Lady Clare," 90.
"Lady of Shalott," 166.
Lamb, Charles, 18, 25.
Lambeth, 74.

Lancelot, 176.
Landor, 124.
"Last of the Barons, The," 73.
"Last Tournament, The," 180.
Laureateship, 89, 154.
Lawrence, Sir Thomas, 73, 74, 113.
Leicester, 109.
Lichfield, 109.
Lincoln, 4, 11.
Lincoln Cathedral, 4.
Lincolnshire, 3, 6, 27, 33, 35, 45, 48, 72, 84, 103, 108, 111.
Lincolnshire Coast, 179.
Lincolnshire Wolds, 49, 65.
Locker-Lampson, Mr., 160.
Lockhart, 65, 101.
"Locksley Hall," 90, 95, 103.
London, 79, 80, 112, 128, 130, 140, 141, 147, 193.
Longfellow, 167.
Lord of Burleigh, 90, 103, 110, 114.
Louth, 6, 44, 45, 97.
Louth Grammar School, 42.
Lushington, Professor E. L., 122, 142, 144.
Lushington, Henry, 121, 145.
Lushingtons, 142.
Lyall, Sir Alfred, 193.
Lythehill, 192.
Lytton, Bulwer, 73.

Mablethorpe, 45, 85.
Macdonald, Dr. George, 136.
Magdalen, 47.

Maidstone, 142.
Maidstone Mechanics' Institute, 145.
Maltby-le-marsh, 46, 85.
"Mariana," 82, 83, 84, 86.
Marmion, Joane de, 98.
Marmion, Philip de, 97.
Marmions, 96, 98.
"Marriage of Geraint, The," 180.
"Maud," 90, 148, 165.
Maurice, 125, 167, 175.
Mavis-Enderby, 35.
"Mayflower," The, 179, 187.
Mead Fields, 186.
"Measure for Measure," 83.
Merivale, 123.
Merlin, 166.
"Miller's Daughter, The," 89, 90, 93, 101, 153.
Milnes, Monckton, 122, 123, 137, 142, 164.
Milton, 123, 124, 190.
Mirehouse, 103.
"Modern Painters," 147, 148.
Montpelier Row, 157.
"Morte d'Arthur," 103, 166.
Moxon, 147.

Needles, The, 181.
New Court, Trinity College, 126.
Nineteenth Century, 189.
North, Christopher, 101.
Northamptonshire, 111.
"Northern Farmer," 88.

INDEX

"Ode on the Death of the Duke of Wellington," 157.
Oldbuck, Jonathan, 35.
Oriel, 47.
Oxford, 47, 123.
Oxfordshire, 156.

"Palace of Art, The," 189.
Palgrave, Professor, 157, 193.
Park House, 142, 145.
Peterhouse, 121.
Pierrepont, Right Hon. Henry Manvers, 114.
Plato, 123.
"Poetry of Sorrow, The," 136.
"Poems by Two Brothers," 44, 58.
"Poems, Chiefly Lyrical," 81, 83, 124.
Pope's Villa, 157.
Prince Albert, 167.
"Princess, The," 145, 189.
Puritans, 24.

Queen Charlotte, 110.
Queen Elizabeth, 111, 112.
Queen Victoria, 89.
"Queen o' the May," 51.
Quirk, Rev. J. F., 60.

Rawnsley, Rev. R. D. B., 156.
Rawnsley, Rev. H. D., 14, 45.
"Recollections of the Arabian Nights," 189.
Reformation, The, 84.

Richard II., 97.
Richmond Road, 157.
Ripon, Bishop of, 193.
Robinson, Rev. G. A., 8.
Rogers, 147.
Rose Crescent, 118.
Ruskin, 4, 103, 147, 149, 190.
Rutland, 111.
Rydal Mount, 176.

Salvator Mundi, 113.
Sandford, Sir Daniel K., 143.
"Scarecrow, or Malkin," 53.
"Scotch Song," 58.
Scotland, 57.
Scott, Sir Walter, 65, 79, 90, 96, 112, 113.
Scrivelsby Court, 96, 98.
Sebastiano del Piombo, 173.
Sellwood, Henry, 56, 155.
Sellwood, Miss Emily Sarah, 155.
Sellwood, Miss Louisa, 50.
Sellwoods, 155.
Severn, 133.
Shakespeare, 25, 83, 173.
Shelley, 87.
Shiplake, 156.
Shiplake Church, 155.
Shotter Mill, 185.
Shropshire, 104.
Simeon, Sir John, 165.
"Sir Launcelot v. Queen Guinevere," 166.
Sir Percivale, 50.

INDEX.

Solent, 163, 178, 179, 187.
Somersby, 5, 6, 7, 10, 11, 14, 16, 27, 29, 33, 34, 38, 41, 42, 43, 45, 64, 65, 84, 85, 87, 92, 93, 95, 96, 124, 128, 130, 137, 139, 150, 155, 171, 179.
Somersby Church, 22, 36, 39.
Somersby Church Bells, 24.
Somersby Church Font, 25.
Somersby Churchyard, 22.
Somersby Cross, 24.
Somersby Grange, 88, 89.
Somersby Register, 25, 26, 27.
Somersby Sundial, 24.
Somersetshire, 155.
Spedding, James, 55, 103, 117, 122.
Spedding, Squire, 65.
Spilsby, 93.
St. Margaret, 36.
St. John's College, 119, 125.
Stamford, 74, 108, 109, 111.
Stanley, Dean, 167.
Sterling, 125.
Stockworth Mill, 88, 94.
Stratford, 26.
"Sunbeam, The," 179.
Surrey, 185, 186, 187.
Sussex, 186.
Swinburne, 180.

Tadema, 187.
Tealby, 48, 66.
Tealby Church, 67, 75.
"Tears, idle tears," 38.

Tennyson, 5, 7, 9, 12, 15, 21, 26, 29, 74, 79, 80, 83, 86, 89, 92, 101, 102, 103, 104, 106, 117, 118, 121, 122, 123, 127, 128, 131, 133, 136, 142, 145, 146, 147, 148, 149, 153, 155, 157, 163, 164, 165, 166, 169, 173, 176, 181, 190.
Tennyson, Lady, 156, 157, 173, 185, 186, 192.
Tennyson, Cecilia, 143.
Tennyson, Charles, 7, 9, 29, 41, 42, 43, 46, 47, 49, 55, 58, 67, 74, 155.
Tennyson, Charlotte, 59.
Tennyson, Edward, 41.
Tennyson, Emilia, 30, 130.
Tennyson, Frederick, 41, 71.
Tennyson, George, 64, 67, 71, 73, 87.
Tennyson, Rev. George Clayton, 6, 7, 12, 14, 24, 27, 28, 29, 36, 37, 124, 189.
Tennyson, Mrs. Elizabeth, 142, 150.
Tennyson, Hon. Hallam, 60, 158, 173.
Tennyson, Hon. Mrs. Hallam, 193.
Tennyson, Horatio, 33, 41, 59.
Tennyson, Lionel, 63, 159, 173.
Tennyson, Mary, 30.
Tennyson, Septimus, 41, 59.
Tennyson, Misses, 37, 85.
Tennysons, 10, 30, 45, 48, 98, 137, 140, 155, 189.

INDEX.

Tennyson's Down, 176.
Tennyson's Lane, 188.
Tent Lodge, **156**.
Thackeray, 6, 122.
Thackeray, Miss, 171, 173.
Thames, 156, 157.
Thirlwall, Bishop, 144.
Thompson, **123**.
Thorpe, John, 111.
"Timbuctoo," 123, 124.
"Times, The," 136.
"To Ulysses," 175.
Trench, 93, 122, 125, 128, 129, 130, 164.
"Tribute, The," 164, 166.
Trinity College, 7, 118, 119, 126, 128, 143.
Trumpington Mill, 93.
Tunbridge Wells, 142.
Turner, 147.
Turner, Miss, 64.
Turner, Rev. Samuel, 48, 49.
Twickenham, 157.
"Two Voices," 21.
Tyndall, 187.

"Ulysses," 102.
Usselby, 64.

Vanbrugh, Sir J., 88.

Venables, 123.
Viceroy of India, **159**.
Vienna, 129, 130.
"**Vision of Sin, The,**" 102.
Vivian, Sir Walter, 189.

Wales, 54.
Waltham Abbey, 138.
Ward, Mrs. Humphry, 187.
Wash, The, 11.
Well Walk, 150.
Wellesley, Lord Charles, 114.
Wellington, Duke of, **114**.
Westminster Hall, 97.
Westmoreland, 3.
"**Westward, Ho!**" 47.
White, Walter, 14.
William the Conqueror, 96.
William IV., 97.
Wilkie, 160.
Wimpole Street, **140**.
Witham Valley, 11.
Woldsby Ebriorum, 51.
Woodbridge, 158.
Wood-Enderby, 35.
Wordsworth, 48, 102, 176.

Yar, 178.
Yarmouth, 163.
Younghusband, Jos., 27.